Instructional Methods for Differentiation & Deeper Learning

James H. **Stronge** Xianxuan **Xu**

Solution Tree | Press

Copyright © 2016 by Solution Tree Press

Materials appearing here are copyrighted. With one exception, all rights are reserved. Readers may reproduce only those pages marked "Reproducible." Otherwise, no part of this book may be reproduced or transmitted in any form or by any means (electronic, photocopying, recording, or otherwise) without prior written permission of the publisher.

555 North Morton Street
Bloomington, IN 47404
800.733.6786 (toll free) / 812.336.7700
FAX: 812.336.7790

email: info@solution-tree.com
solution-tree.com

Visit **go.solution-tree.com/instruction** to download the reproducibles in this book.

Printed in the United States of America

19 18 17 16 15   1 2 3 4 5

Library of Congress Cataloging-in-Publication Data

Stronge, James H.
  Instructional methods for differentiation and deeper learning / James H. Stronge and Xianxuan Xu.
      pages cm
  Includes bibliographical references and index.
  ISBN 978-1-942496-53-3 (perfect bound) 1. Individualized instruction--United States. 2. Mixed ability grouping in education--United States. 3. Effective teaching I. Xu, Xianxuan. II. Title.
  LB1031.S78 2016
  371.39'4--dc23
                                    2015030467

Solution Tree

Jeffrey C. Jones, CEO
Edmund M. Ackerman, President

Solution Tree Press

President: Douglas M. Rife
Senior Acquisitions Editor: Amy Rubenstein
Editorial Director: Lesley Bolton
Managing Production Editor: Caroline Weiss
Production Editor: Rachel Rosolina
Copy Editor: Miranda Addonizio
Proofreader: Elisabeth Abrams
Text and Cover Designer: Rian Anderson
Compositor: Laura Kagemann

Acknowledgments

Solution Tree Press would like to thank the following reviewers:

Melissa Jordan
Science Teacher
Sarah Scott Middle School
Terre Haute, Indiana

Charles Maranzano Jr.
Superintendent
Vernon Township School District
Vernon, New Jersey

Debbie Schuler
Administrator of Instructional Services
Florida School for the Deaf and the Blind
St. Augustine, Florida

Visit **go.solution-tree.com/instruction** to download the reproducibles in this book.

Table of Contents

Reproducible pages are in italics.

About the Authors ix
Introduction 1
    Differentiation 1
    Deeper Learning 1
    An Overview of the Book 2
    Summary: So Where Do We Go From Here? 2

Part I
Differentiated Instructional Methods for Effective Teaching 5

Chapter 1
Delivering Differentiated Remedial Instruction 7
    What Research Says About Delivering Differentiated Remedial Instruction 7
    How to Move From Research to Practice 9
    Summary 12
    Identify Weaknesses in Student Learning 13
    Delivering Differentiated and Tiered Instruction 15
    Student Affect 16

Chapter 2
Delivering Differentiated Instruction for Gifted Students 17
    What Research Says About Delivering Differentiated Learning for
        Gifted Students 18
    How to Move From Research to Practice 19
    Summary 21
    Differentiation Lesson Plan 23
    Self-Assessment Checklist 24
    Research-Supported Practices in Gifted Education 26

Chapter 3
Delivering Differentiated Instruction for Culturally and Linguistically Diverse Students 27
    What Research Says About Delivering Differentiated Instruction for Culturally
        and Linguistically Diverse Students 28
    How to Move From Research to Practice 29
    Summary 30
    Teacher Reflection 32
    Culturally Responsive Instruction 33
    Student Learning Profile 34

Part II
Deeper Learning Methods for Effective Teaching 35

Chapter 4
Questioning 37
What Research Says About Questioning 37
How to Move From Research to Practice 39
Summary 40
Questioning Technique Analysis *44*
Good Questioning Practices Checklist *45*
Questioning for the Learning Domains *46*
Student-Developed Questioning *48*
Content-Focused Questions Design Form *49*

Chapter 5
Metacognition 51
What Research Says About Metacognition 51
How to Move From Research to Practice 52
Summary 55
Encouraging Students to Think About Thinking *56*
Encouraging Students to Ask Metacognitive Questions *57*
Teacher Self-Assessment of Metacognition Use *58*

Chapter 6
Creativity 59
What Research Says About Creativity 59
How to Move From Research to Practice 60
Summary 62
Self-Assessment of Creativity *63*
Promoting Creativity Through Creative Processes *64*
Incorporating Creativity Into the Lesson *65*
Measuring Creativity *68*

Chapter 7
Critical Thinking 69
What Research Says About Critical Thinking 70
How to Move From Research to Practice 71
Summary 73
Questions That Make Students Mindful *75*
Student Self-Assessment of Disposition and Metacognition in Critical Thinking ... *78*
Checklist of Critical-Thinking Skills *79*

Chapter 8
Complex Thinking 81
What Research Says About Complex Thinking 81
How to Move From Research to Practice 83
Summary 85
Deepen the Instruction *86*
Strategy Reflection Activity *88*
The ABC List *89*
Teacher Self-Assessment *90*

Chapter 9
Active Learning 93
    What Research Says About Active Learning 94
    How to Move From Research to Practice 94
    Summary 97
    Self-Assessment of Active Learning *98*
    Learning Activities *100*
    Planning for Student Active Learning *101*

Chapter 10
Problem-Based Learning 103
    What Research Says About Problem-Based Learning 103
    How to Move From Research to Practice 104
    Summary 106
    Teacher Scaffolding *107*
    Process Worksheet *109*
    Teacher Self-Assessment Checklist *111*

References and Resources 113
Index 127

About the Authors

James H. Stronge, PhD, is president of Stronge and Associates Educational Consulting, an educational consulting company that focuses on teacher and leader effectiveness with projects internationally and in many U.S. states. Additionally, he is the Heritage Professor of Education, a distinguished professorship in the Educational Policy, Planning, and Leadership program at the College of William and Mary in Williamsburg, Virginia.

Dr. Stronge's research interests include policy and practice related to teacher effectiveness, teacher and administrator evaluation, and teacher selection. He has worked with state departments of education, school districts, and U.S. and international education organizations to design and implement evaluation and hiring systems for teachers, administrators, and support personnel. Recently, he completed work on new teacher and principal evaluation systems for American international schools in conjunction with the Association of American Schools in South America and supported by the U.S. Department of State. Dr. Stronge has made more than 350 presentations at regional, national, and international conferences and has conducted workshops for education organizations extensively throughout the U.S. and internationally. Among his current research projects are international comparative studies of national award-winning teachers in the United States and China and influences of economic and societal trends on student academic performance in countries globally.

Dr. Stronge has authored, coauthored, or edited twenty-six books and approximately two hundred articles, chapters, and technical reports. His 1994 book, *Educating Homeless Children and Adolescents: Evaluating Policy and Practice* received the Outstanding Academic Book Award from the American Library Association.

Dr. Stronge was a founding member of the board of directors for the Consortium for Research on Educational Accountability and Teacher Evaluation (CREATE). In 2011, he was honored with the Frank E. Flora Lamp of Knowledge Award, presented by the Virginia Association of Secondary School Principals for "bringing honor to the profession" and his "record of outstanding contributions." He was selected as the 2012 national recipient of the Millman Award from CREATE in recognition of his work in the field of teacher and administrator evaluation.

Xianxuan Xu, PhD, is a senior research associate at Stronge and Associates Educational Consulting. Dr. Xu received her doctorate from the College of William and Mary's Educational Policy, Planning, and Leadership program. Her research interests are teacher effectiveness, professional development, and teacher and principal evaluation. She is also particularly interested in researching the relationship between culture and education issues such as teaching, learning, and leadership. She has presented research findings at various U.S. conferences, including the American Educational Research Association, University Council for Educational Administration, and National Evaluation Institute. She is also a contributing author to *Principal Evaluation: Standards, Rubrics, and Tools for Effective Performance* and *West Meets East: Best Practices From Expert Teachers in the U.S. and China.*

Visit www.strongeandassociates.com to learn more about Dr. Stronge and Dr. Xu's work.

To book James H. Stronge or Xianxuan Xu for professional development, please contact pd@solution-tree.com.

Introduction

Portions of this material appear in Stronge, Grant, and Xu (2015).

Sometimes classrooms seem like isolated, black boxes. To discover what makes a teacher effective, we need to look into the black box of the classroom and see how teachers translate their content knowledge, pedagogical skills, and resources into opportunities for student learning. In essence, quality instruction counts; *how* teachers instruct plays a powerful and lasting role in student learning and success.

We have the chapters on instructional delivery organized into two books. The first, *Instructional Strategies for Effective Teaching* (Stronge & Xu, 2016), provides a variety of well-established strategies of teaching, which not only have a strong rationale but also are backed up by lines of research regarding their impact, how they work, and in what scenarios they work best. They form a foundation for quality teaching. There is not a single instructional strategy that can serve as a magical silver bullet and work for all types of learning objectives; instead, effective teaching calls on a broad repertoire of strategies and involves dynamic interactions among content to be learned, pedagogical methods applied, and needs of individual learners.

The second, *Instructional Methods for Differentiation and Deeper Learning* focuses on two distinguishing features of excellent teaching: (1) differentiation and (2) deeper learning. Instead of discussing instructional strategies one by one, this book organizes ideas and practices that cross approaches or models of teaching. These chapters help teachers and instructional leaders think about the needs of students and better understand the strategies in *Instructional Strategies for Effective Teaching* and how to use them to the best benefit of student learning. The strategies presented in *Instructional Strategies for Effective Teaching* are adaptable. Teachers should validate and adjust the methods in their specific classrooms. This book, while still providing standalone teaching skills and strategies, can be considered as necessary and, thus, more mandatory to providing the best instruction to all students. Let's take a closer look at each.

Differentiation

Students come to the classroom varying in culture, socioeconomic status, interests, and abilities. Instead of using uniform strategies for all students, effective teachers design instruction that motivates each student and builds on prior learning and individual ability. The benefits of this approach are great. Adeptly implementing a variety of classroom techniques and strategies enhances student motivation and decreases discipline problems (Dolezal, Welsh, Pressley, & Vincent, 2003).

Differentiated instruction enables teachers to address learner variance by adjusting curriculum, materials, learning activities, learning environment, and assessments. It provides students with optimal avenues to process new knowledge and develop skills according to their readiness and interest, while enjoying equal access to high-quality learning (Tomlinson, 2003).

Deeper Learning

Researchers expect employment in the professional, scientific, technical, and computer systems fields to increase by 45 percent between 2010 and 2018 (U.S. Department of Labor, 2010), and this trend is likely to continue. These fields rely heavily on logic, reasoning, and critical thinking. Thus, business leaders, policymakers, and educators have begun to recognize the development and transfer of complex thinking skills as primary goals for education. Education expert Tony Wagner (2008a, 2008b) has conducted conversations with several hundred business, nonprofit, philanthropic, and education leaders and conducted walkthroughs of classrooms in some of the most highly regarded public schools in the United States. He discovered a disconcerting gap between the qualities that students need to become productive citizens in the 21st century (such as critical thinking skills, problem solving, collaboration, leadership, adaptability, entrepreneurialism, creativity, effective communication, curiosity, and imagination) and the schooling the students are getting (passive learning environments and uninspired lessons that focus on test preparation and reward memorization). He notes that this problem exists in low-performing *and* high-performing schools.

Beyond this disconnect of expectations, however, effective teachers are aware that brain researchers consider students to be optimized for the development of higher-order cognitive processes. They care about students' ability to transfer learning into out-of-school and other real-world contexts. They focus on meaningful conceptualization of knowledge and skills rather than on isolated facts (Fullan & Langworthy, 2013; Rogers-Chapman & Darling-Hammond, 2013; Wenglinsky, 2004). They provide in-depth explanations of academic content and cover higher-order concepts and skills thoroughly (Wenglinsky, 2004). Again, the benefits are high; Robert Sternberg (2003) finds that elementary and middle school students who receive instruction emphasizing both critical thinking *and* memorization perform better on academic achievement tests than students in classrooms where instruction emphasizes critical thinking *or* memorization.

An Overview of the Book

Because differentiation and deeper learning are so important to effective instruction, each chapter in this book focuses on an important aspect of these two instructional delivery methods. The three chapters in part I focus on differentiation. Chapter 1 is about delivering differentiated remedial instruction. Chapter 2 covers delivering differentiated instruction for gifted students. Finally, chapter 3 details delivering differentiated instruction for culturally and linguistically diverse students.

Part II consists of chapters 4 through 10, which address the following aspects of cognitive challenge: questioning, metacognition, creativity, critical thinking, complex thinking, active learning, and problem-based learning.

To make the book relevant and useful, each chapter includes the following sections.

- An introduction to the instructional method
- What research says about the instructional method
- How to move from research to practice

To end each chapter, we include several handouts to help teachers use these instructional methods immediately. Our intent is for teachers and school leaders to take the methods they find useful right off of the page and put them into practice as seamlessly as possible.

Teachers can use many of the featured methods for self-assessment and reflection. They are also useful for administrators to assess instructional practices from the formative perspective. As summarized in table I.1, we support three specific groups of educators in the important work of delivering effective teaching.

Table I.1: Goals for Each Audience

Audience	Goals of Book
Teachers improving practice	• Self-reflection • Guided study • Teacher-directed growth
Teachers teaching teachers	• Mentor tips • Instructional coaching tips • Peer networks
Leaders supporting teachers	• Directed growth • Supervisor support for teachers • Coordinated curriculum

Summary: So Where Do We Go From Here?

Our goals for this book include improving, supporting, and sustaining student learning with high-quality instructional delivery. The focus of this book is on providing the instruction that students really need—differentiated instruction and instruction that fosters deeper learning—to be successful in not just learning subject-specific knowledge in the classroom but also developing skills they need to address the pressing problems in the 21st century. The chapters in this book represent the idea that quality instruction is a continuous endeavor of refining practice to identify the optimal level of challenge in learning tasks, increase the rigor of learning, and enhance engagement of students in the learning process. We hope you find this guide on instructional methods practical, solidly researched, and easy to use. Now, let's put these methods to use in your school or classroom.

Part I

Differentiated Instructional Methods for Effective Teaching

Teachers report that meeting the needs of students with a wide range of learning abilities and backgrounds is one of the greatest challenges they encounter in the classroom. The low self-efficacy related to differentiation has to do with the perceived lack of knowledge and skill about adapting curriculum materials and adjusting instructional strategies efficiently and effectively during the flow of teaching and learning (Tobin & Tippett, 2014). When differentiating instruction, the teacher uses multiple, flexible instructional materials, activities, and assessment techniques so that there are options for students engaging in learning. It also maximizes outcomes.

In order to make differentiated instruction more manageable and practicable, the three chapters in part I approach differentiation from the following perspectives: delivering differentiated remedial instruction, delivering differentiated instruction for gifted students, and delivering differentiated instruction for culturally and linguistically diverse students. The core information running through these chapters is that instead of using one-size-fits-all strategies for all students, teachers can use differentiated instruction to communicate content and skills in a way that makes them accessible to students based on their individual prior learnings and abilities. Differentiated instruction involves recognizing and acting on students' diversity of readiness, prior knowledge, and interests to enhance each student's growth through diverse materials and optimal support.

Chapter 1
Delivering Differentiated Remedial Instruction

In an ideal world, every student would (and should) be able to succeed, even if it is at different rates and with different strengths. To differentiate instruction is to recognize an individual student's learning history, background, readiness to learn, interests, and acquired skill set, and then choose instructional strategies more tailored to that student, or a small group, to speed academic success. Converting the school mission statement from "We believe that all children can learn" to "We expect all children to learn" would be a major step in this direction.

With this perspective in mind, consider the following quote:

> Every child can learn. That so many students fail to attain necessary skills reflects not the incapacity of the students but the incapacity of schools to meet the needs of every child. Given a skilled one-to-one tutor, for example, every student without severe dyslexia or retardation could attain an adequate level of basic skills. Practically speaking, of course, it is unlikely that we will soon be providing a skilled tutor for every child who is falling behind in reading or math. Nevertheless, we can develop feasible programs to ensure that every child learns. The first step is to consider what we know about practices that can accelerate the achievement of students in danger of school failure. (Slavin & Madden, 1989, p. 4)

Although Robert Slavin and Nancy Madden stated this in the late 1980s, their ideas are still relevant.

Teachers should use remedial instruction for any students, with or without special needs, who have not reached the goal. Remediation does not necessarily mean summer school or afterschool tutoring. Instead, teachers can incorporate it into daily instruction as they use student learning data to decide who needs additional support and what strategies to use. It should serve as an ongoing proactive component of instruction to catch students before they fall too far behind. In order to close the achievement gaps that persist in the education system, it is critical for teachers to consider how to help low-achieving students improve their learning. So how can teachers enhance opportunities for struggling students to maximize learning? This chapter focuses on delivering effective instruction in remedial settings. In this chapter, *differentiated remedial instruction* refers to the intervention practices that teachers use to track individual student performance and bridge the learning gaps for students who are falling behind their peers.

What Research Says About Delivering Differentiated Remedial Instruction

A meta-analysis on teaching remedial reading to adolescents, with or without reading disabilities, shows that instruction in comprehension significantly improves students' comprehension skills, with an average effect size of 1.23 (an increase of 39 percentile points) (Edmonds et al., 2009). In another study on reading, Lisa Limbrick, Kevin Wheldall, and Alison Madelaine (2012) find that remedial instruction has effect size gains ranging from 0.83 to 1.21 for boys and 0.85 to 1.25 for girls (an increase of 30 to 39 percentile points) on various aspects of effective reading. Similar positive impact of remedial instruction was also found in the subject area of mathematics. Fuchs and colleagues (2009) find that remedial instruction explicitly targeting students' specific learning difficulties with mathematics (such as mathematics difficulty alone versus mathematics plus reading difficulty) has an effect size of 0.79 on the learning outcomes (an increase of 29 percentile points).

A major implication of this line of research is that teachers need to continuously diagnose student learning and make this diagnosis an integral part of decision making in designing remedial instruction for students, especially for students who are at risk of low achievement. One way to accomplish this remediation is to use Bloom's mastery learning—an instructional model that breaks learning content down into several small segments and allows students time to acquire the prerequisite knowledge or skill before moving to new learning (Bloom, 1984). Hunter Boylan and D. Patrick Saxon (1999) define *mastery learning* as small steps of instruction, frequent assessment, and empowerment of students to master learning materials in a progressive, logical manner. These frequent checks for understanding pinpoint student confusion and give teachers a direction for further instruction. Furthermore, mastery learning not only has positive effects on students' learning performance (Wambugu & Changeiywo, 2008) but also enhances students' motivation toward learning by raising their expectancies of success in academic work and correcting their area of weakness, thus breaking the cycle of failure (Changeiywo, Wambugu, & Wachanga, 2011). After all, positive student affect plays an important role in the success of remedial instruction. Consider the following (Crumpton, 2011; Hasan & Khalid, 2014).

- Research indicates that low-achieving learners are more likely to display deficient attitudes toward learning, self-perception, and self-regulation.
- Low-achieving students can be defined as those who are falling behind but have no learning disabilities.
- Underachievement refers to a discrepancy between potential and actual performance.
- Underachievers are students who appear to be capable of succeeding in learning but are nonetheless struggling.

Another way to accomplish remediation, according to Paul McDermott and Marley Watkins (1983), is to incorporate the following attributes into instruction to benefit struggling students.

- Frequent and immediate feedback
- Individualized pacing and programming
- Modularized and hierarchical curriculum
- Outcomes stated as performance objectives
- A mastery learning paradigm
- Clarity of presentation
- Motivation
- A multisensory learning format
- Personalized instruction

These critical elements provide the major building blocks for effective remediation for students who encounter difficulties in learning. Instruction with these attributes holds the potential to bridge the gap for students who may be at risk of failure and ensures delivery of carefully tailored supplemental interventions.

Interestingly, the research synthesis by Slavin and Madden (1989) finds that supplementary or remedial instructional strategies that show evidence of effectiveness generally fall into two major categories: (1) remedial tutoring programs and (2) computer-assisted instruction. Tutoring is probably the most extensive mode of supplemental support for at-risk students. It is generally considered the most powerful form of instruction for increasing underachieving students' academic performance (Bloom, 1984; Elbaum, Vaughn, Hughes, & Moody, 2000). One-to-one instruction is validated by research to be an effective way of increasing student achievement, especially for students who are considered at risk of academic failure (Osborn et al., 2007). A key element of successful tutoring is tailoring instruction to meet individual student needs (Elbaum et al., 2000). If instructors other than the classroom teachers are the ones providing the tutoring, then it is essential for them to continuously collaborate with the students' classroom teachers to make the tutoring effective (Gordon, 2009).

Regarding computer-assisted instruction, a study by Nina Saine, Marja-Kristiina Lerkkanen, Timo Ahonen, Asko Tolvanen, and Heikki Lyytinen (2010) finds that such interventions could increase seven-year-old elementary school beginners' reading fluency. The heart of computer-assisted remedial reading instruction lies in its capacity to enrich regular remedial reading intervention by providing an intensive learning environment with individualized repetition of drill and practice. It also provides prompt visual and audio feedback for students' correct and incorrect choices on letter-sound relations. The study finds that computer-assisted instruction can help students with deficits (the lowest achieving 30 percent of students) in core prereading skills (such as letter knowledge, phonological awareness, or rapid automatized naming) reach the average reading level of the mainstream group by the end of grade 2. Computer-assisted intervention has an effect size of 1.01 (an increase of 19 percentile points) on student reading fluency and 2.08 (2.08!, an increase of 50 percentile points!) on letter knowledge compared with regular remedial reading interventions.

Additionally, Chun-Hung Lin and colleagues (2013) find that game-based and video-based remedial instruction incorporated with elements of mastery learning can improve mathematics learning for students with low achievement. In this study, the researchers incorporated content related to the area of a circle into a computer-based Monopoly game. Throughout the game, the students received immediate remedial instruction (they choose to watch an instructional video and review the supplementary materials as many times as they need) specifically for the questions they were unable to answer correctly. The findings indicate the game-based remedial instruction has an effect size of 0.47; in other words, it can improve students' learning outcomes by about 18 percentile points.

How to Move From Research to Practice

Many students become chronic underachievers, not because they lack learning capability, but because teachers don't fully accommodate their individual learning needs in the classroom and other learning situations. One approach to conducting remedial instruction is to vary and adapt instructional approaches in relation to individual differences, rather than duplicating the original instruction designed for the whole class. Teachers need to be aware that without thoughtful planning for real adjustment in their instruction, one-to-one tutoring, pull-out special education instruction, reteaching, and any other type of remedial instruction are likely to be ineffective. As a result, these at-risk students tend to fail again when they attempt to learn the same content or skill a second time.

Drawing from a meta-review of the extant research on teacher effectiveness, Stronge and colleagues provide guidance for effectively implementing instruction for at-risk students (Stronge, Ward, Tucker, & Hindman, 2007).

- Expect students to do their work, and do not accept excuses.
- Be on task every minute in the classroom, and make sure students have time to learn.
- Examine the nature of the lesson and cultural assumptions that negatively affect at-risk students.
- Focus on understanding rather than isolated facts.
- Use pacing guides and timelines in order to align the instruction and learning with the curriculum.
- Plan for a variety of activities, including individualized instruction, student-led activities, student-centered learning time, and an infusion of technology, if available.

Instead of providing low-achieving students with a rigorous, challenging curriculum and encouragement for learning, teachers are inclined to expect less from them. The vicious cycle of low expectations and low performance perpetuates when students are considered less able and less teachable and are required to read less and recall only simple facts, while high-performing students are challenged to engage in advanced cognitive learning. Holding high performance expectations impacts teachers' instructional practices and their interactions with students, consciously or unconsciously. When teachers hold themselves and every student accountable to reasonable anticipations about growth, they are more likely to provide meaningful learning experiences and an instructional foundation for students to be successful.

The beliefs teachers have about their students' abilities to learn can positively or negatively impact students' actual learning. For instance, teacher perceptions and expectations are expressed through the type of goals teachers set for students, the skills and resources used during instruction, and the types of reinforcement used in the classroom (Ferguson, 1998; Sakiz, Pape, & Hoy, 2012). Teachers with low expectations and lack of efficacy often lower the academic rigor, invest less teacher effort, and use watered-down curriculum for low-achieving students, especially in poor, urban schools (Kelly & Carbonaro, 2012; Rubie-Davies, Flint, & McDonald, 2012; Warren, 2002).

Students who are the target of teachers' low expectations are given fewer opportunities to learn new materials than peers with high expectations. For instance, the wait time to answer a question is less than that allotted for high-expectation students. Low-expectation students are often given the answers to questions directly, or the teacher calls on other students rather than giving them clues or repeating or rephrasing questions, as is done with high-expectation students. Low-expectation students also tend to receive inappropriate feedback, such as more frequent and severe criticism for failure and insincere praise. They also endure less-friendly and less-responsive classroom interactions (such as less smiling, affirmative head nodding, leaning forward, or eye contact). Teachers also provide brief and less-informative feedback, or less-stimulating and more lower-cognitive-level questions. These practices impact students' achievement, academic engagement, and motivation (Cotton, 1989; Sorhagen, 2013).

Students often recognize teacher bias and conform to teacher expectations—a phenomenon called *self-fulfilling prophecy*. Children, from their early years in school, are highly sensitive to differential teacher expectations and behavior, and this sensitivity cuts across grades, gender, and ability levels. George Kuh (2003) states:

> Students typically don't exceed their own expectation, particularly with regard to academic work. But students will go beyond what they think they can do under certain conditions, one of which is that their teachers expect, challenge, and support them to do so. (p. 28)

Students are more engaged with their learning when they perceive high expectations of the teachers and believe that academic learning will enable them to do something positive in their lives. Christine Rubie-Davies (2006) finds that in a single school year, students' self-perceptions of abilities in academic learning can be altered substantially in line with teachers' expectations. The core tenet of remedial instruction, or instruction in general, is the belief that all students can learn and succeed, and in some cases, they just need support and assistance beyond the norm.

Slavin and Madden (1989) also enumerate key attributes of effective remedial instruction. According to them, the instruction requires good planning and comprehensive approaches. That means the productive remedial instruction always includes detailed specific curriculum standards, lesson plans, and supportive materials. Effective remedial instruction involves systematic and carefully constructed alternative learning opportunities, rather than just a one-time dose of extra exposure to the learning content by happenstance. Any additional instruction for remediation needs to be intensive and target specific areas, based on the results of frequent assessment. Teachers should adapt their instruction style, such as modifying groupings, based on these assessment results.

After synthesizing thirty years of research from the 1960s to the 1990s, Boylan and Saxon (1999) note that effective remediation establishes clearly defined goals and objectives for improved student performance. To effectively remediate, teachers must provide a high degree of structure for student compensatory learning; this can require teachers to build an organizational schema to help students fully comprehend the necessary academic concepts. Teachers can do this through providing highly structured learning experiences, such as modeling appropriate methods of organizing information. Boylan and Saxon (1999) also note that teachers should use a wide variety of teaching approaches and methods, such as class discussion and group projects, so that students can choose modes of learning that are most meaningful and relevant to them.

Regardless of the method a teacher chooses, it takes time and effort to implement remediation, especially considering the original reason for low achievement. Edward Daly, Joseph Witt, Brian Martens, and Eric Dool (1997) propose a model with five types of interventions to address the various reasons for student failure. They hypothesize that the easiest intervention is motivational and the hardest intervention is changing the instructional level to match the student's performance level. See table 1.1 for Daly et al.'s (1997) recommended instructional strategies for each type of intervention.

Pulling all the ideas together, remedial instruction is a form of differentiated instruction applied in addition to regular classroom teaching and targeting students who are already behind their peers. Students fall behind for a myriad of cognitive, affective, or social reasons. It behooves teachers to assess and diagnose the problems in student learning and continuously adapt instruction to meet individual needs.

Table 1.1: Samples of remediation and strategies for improvement.

Why Students Fail	Type of Intervention	Evidence-Based Strategies to Implement the Intended Intervention
They do not want to do it.	There are performance deficits (rather than skill deficits). They need intervention involving motivation.	• Offer incentives. • Offer a choice of work to perform. • Offer a choice of instructional activities.
They have not spent enough time doing it.	They need intervention involving meaningful learning opportunities.	• Use observation to estimate the student's academically engaged time in the problematic subject area. • Increase active engagement by providing highly structured tasks, allocating sufficient time for instruction, providing continuous and active instruction, decreasing intrusions (such as transition time), maintaining high success rates, and providing immediate feedback.
They have not had enough help to do it.	They need intervention involving modified instructional practices.	• Carefully consider a student's skill level, and develop a sequence of stages to specify what and how much assistance students need to achieve proficiency. • Use the skill across time and contexts. • Initially, model the skill with the student observing. Immediate and explicit corrective feedback is critical to ensure the accuracy of performance. • Once students have achieved accuracy, incorporate practice and reinforcement into the instruction to promote fluency in skill performance.
They have not had to do it that way before. (For instance, students might not be spending time on the right kinds of instructional activities that lead to mastery.)	They need intervention involving instructional materials, tasks, and assignments.	• Explicitly define learning objectives. • Improve instructional materials, activities, and assignments to elicit the kinds of performance that teachers expect of students who have mastered the curriculum. • Provide enough practice in actual use of the skill.
It is too hard.	They need intervention involving instructional materials, tasks, and assignments.	• Modify instructional materials, tasks, and assignments to ensure they are at the same level as students' skill levels.

Source: Daly et al., 1997.

Summary

Several themes emerged from the discussions on remedial instruction, such as tutoring, individualized interventions based on student area of weakness, diagnostic assessment, and progress monitoring. We have observed underachieving students fall into the self-reinforcing cycle of failure with increasing gaps in achievement as they move from lower grades to higher grades. Teachers cannot afford to wait until the students are already one or two years behind the peers to bring in the remedial instruction. By then, even the most effective intervention would fall short of bridging the gap. Intensive and systematic remedial instruction should be a steady complement to regular classroom instruction and should be provided immediately when students show signs of not mastering the basic skills. To close, we provide several handouts to assist teachers in their journeys toward effective remedial instruction.

The handout "Identify Weaknesses in Student Learning" is based on the work of Paul Bambrick-Santoyo (2010) and extends his reflection template. It aims to help teachers and students collaboratively identify any areas of weakness in understanding and make remedial instruction a data-driven process.

The handout "Delivering Differentiated and Tiered Instruction" (page 15) draws on Dunn and Dunn's learning style model (as cited in Dunn & Honigsfeld, 2009) to help teachers design remedial instruction that provides environment, methods, and materials aligned with student needs and learning styles.

The final handout, "Student Affect" (page 16), is a student survey that helps teachers evaluate students' learning affects in a variety of domains. These data can inform teachers regarding how to address students' attitudes while improving their academic learning.

Identify Weaknesses in Student Learning

Student: _____

Quiz Questions	Learning Objectives What Knowledge or Skill Was Tested?	Did You Get the Question Right or Wrong?		What Was the Reason That You Got the Question Wrong?	
		Right	Wrong	Careless Mistake	Don't Know How to Solve
1.					
2.					
3.					
4.					
5.					
6.					
7.					
8.					
9.					
10.					

The teacher completes the following section after compiling the data from the student section.

1. List the quiz questions on which more than 20 percent of students indicate, "Don't Know How to Solve."

2. Describe the remedial instruction to deliver for corresponding learning objectives.

3. Design similar but different quiz questions.

4. Reassess and analyze the data again to see if students have mastered the learning objectives after the remedial instruction.

Source: Adapted from Bambrick-Santoyo, P. (2010). Driven by data: A practical guide to improve instruction. San Francisco: Jossey-Bass.

Delivering Differentiated and Tiered Instruction

Learning style is the way students concentrate on, process, internalize, and remember academic information.

Dimension	Elements	Use the following questions to consider your students' learning styles, especially those who are struggling academically.	What adjustments could you make for remedial instruction?
Environment	• Sound • Light • Temperature • Seating design	• Are the students distracted by noise or quietness? • Do students prefer a brightly lit, warm environment or a subdued, cooler environment? • Should the learning environment be formal (desks and chairs) or informal (pillows and rugs)?	
Emotional	• Motivation • Responsibility • Task persistence • Structure	• Do students need a lot of emotional support? • Are they persistent with learning tasks? • Can they assume individual responsibility? • Do they need lots of imposed structure, or do they prefer personal options?	
Sociological	• Self • Pair • Team • Adult • Varied	• Do students learn best individually or by working with peers? • How much guidance from adults do they want or need? • Do students prefer to learn in a variety of ways or in certain patterns or routines?	
Physiological	• Perceptual • Intake • Mobility • Time of day	• Are the students auditory, visual, tactual, or kinesthetic learners? • Do the students like to snack while concentrating? • When is the optimal time for learning particular content or skills? • Do the students learn best when they have the freedom to move during learning?	
Psychological	• Analytical • Global • Reflective • Impulsive	• How do the students attack problems—globally (looking at the big picture) or analytically (addressing individual elements of a problem separately)? • Do the students jump into problems or pause to reflect and plan before starting?	

Source: Adapted from Dunn, R., & Honigsfeld, A. (2009). Differentiating instruction for at-risk students: What to do and how to do it. Lanham, MD: Rowman & Littlefield.

Instructional Methods for Differentiation and Deeper Learning © 2016 Solution Tree Press • solution-tree.com
Visit **go.solution-tree.com/instruction** to download this page.

Student Affect

Student: _____

	To a Great Extent	Somewhat	Very Little	Not at All
Self-Concept and Self-Efficacy				
It is easy for me to communicate my thoughts and ideas.				
I can do almost all the academic work if I try hard enough.				
Learning ability is something that I can change.				
Self-Motivation				
When my solution to a task is not working, I try to figure out what went wrong and try alternative solutions.				
Setbacks				
I believe it is satisfying and rewarding to invest effort in understanding the content as thoroughly as possible.				
If my quiz score for the class is sliding, I will study harder instead of ignoring my problems.				
Self-Regulation				
I take responsibility for working toward my goals.				
I do not procrastinate, and I complete my work on time.				
I am good at concentrating on my work.				
I can calm myself down when I am excited or upset.				
I keep my assignments, class notes, and old quizzes in one place so that I can review them when necessary.				
Attitude Toward Learning				
I believe learning is important to my success in life.				
I learn because of interests, curiosity, and enjoyment.				
I regularly set goals and objectives for my learning.				

Chapter 2

Delivering Differentiated Instruction for Gifted Students

Data from both the 2009 and 2012 Programme for International Student Assessment (PISA) show that the United States is behind other leading countries in producing high-achieving students (Organisation for Economic Co-operation and Development [OECD], 2009, 2012). While the proportion of top reading and science performers among all test-takers in the United States is around the OECD (2012) average, the United States has proportionally fewer students reaching advanced achievement levels in mathematics compared to other industrialized nations, as indicated in figure 2.1. Specifically, only 2 percent of U.S. students reach the highest level (level 6) of performance in mathematics (the OECD average is 3 percent), compared with 31 percent of students in Shanghai, China. Typically, students in level 6 can develop and work with models for complex situations and strategically use broad, well-developed thinking and reasoning skills.

Some good news for the United States is that education initiatives since the 1970s have focused substantially on bridging the gap for low-performing students and setting benchmarks for all students, as discussed in chapter 1. Unfortunately, the same focus doesn't exist for gifted or high-performing students (Greene & Cross, 2013; Konstantopoulos, Modi, & Hedges, 2001). Do note that gifted students can be defined in many ways, and we adopt the most widely accepted definition from the U.S. Department of Education: "Children and youth with outstanding talent who perform or show potential for performing

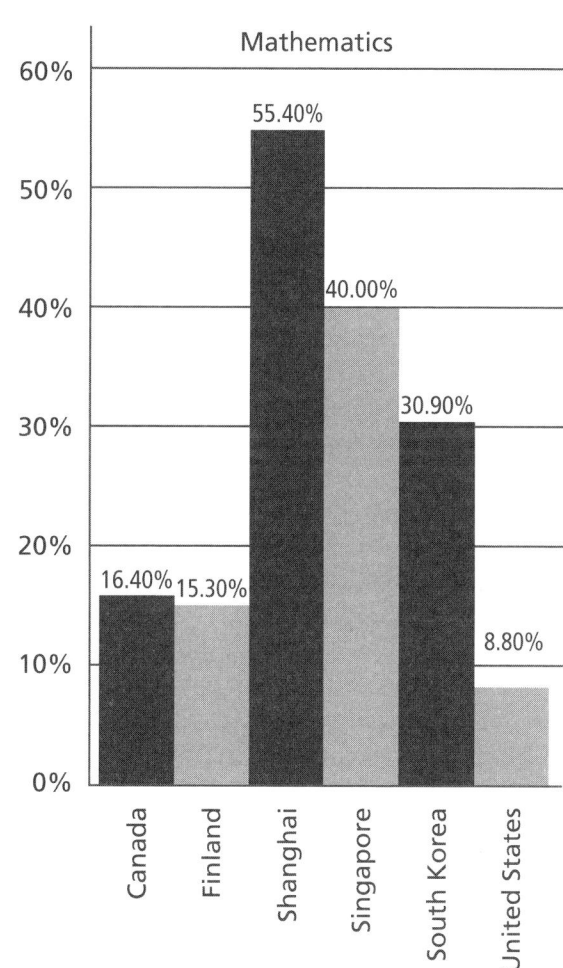

Source: Data from OECD, 2014.

Figure 2.1: PISA 2012 data—Share of top-performing students in mathematics (reaching PISA level 5 and level 6).

at remarkably high level accomplishments when compared with others of their age, experience, or environment" (National Society for the Gifted and Talented, 2015, p. 1). In other words, giftedness does not only speak of talent, but also the performance and accomplishment.

The Common Core State Standards (National Governors Association Center for Best Practices [NGA] & Council of Chief State School Officers [CCSSO], 2010a, 2010b) are reasonably rigorous and a major step toward raising the bar for students, but given their grade specificity, they will not be sufficient for the most advanced students. Consider the following findings regarding gifted learners.

- Above-average students are the last to benefit from increases in the level of teacher effectiveness (Sanders & Horn, 1998), and it is a common pattern for "the best students to make the lowest gains" (Wright, Horn, & Sanders, 1997, p. 65).

- There is no curricular or instructional differentiation for high-ability students in 84 percent of learning activities in regular classrooms (Westberg, Archambault, Dobyns, & Salvin, 1993).

- Compared with high-achieving learners, low-achieving students are more likely to be the top priority of teachers, with 81 percent of the teachers in one study stating that they tend to give one-on-one attention to academically struggling students, but only 5 percent give such attention to advanced students (Loveless, Farkas, & Duffett, 2008).

So what should teachers do to enhance the learning opportunities and success of high-performing students? One clear and compelling answer is to provide them with a fair opportunity for an education that fits their learning abilities and levels. In other words, deliver differentiated learning opportunities that challenge and encourage these gifted students.

What Research Says About Delivering Differentiated Learning for Gifted Students

In many studies, effectiveness in teaching gifted learners is related to teachers' competence in selecting appropriate high-level materials that match task complexities and individual skills (Callahan, Moon, Oh, Azano, & Hailey, 2015; Robinson, Dailey, Hughes, & Cotabish, 2014). For instance, Ben Graffam (2006) finds that exemplary teachers of gifted learners facilitate student-centered classrooms, in which the students help make decisions about curriculum design and have some choice regarding learning objectives, tasks, assignments, and learning products. These teachers also did the following.

- Developed both self-directed and cooperative learning within the classroom, thus framing independent and group learning simultaneously

- Skillfully used differentiation, acceleration, and compacting to deliver an individualized curriculum for their high achievers (compacting is a strategy to replace regular learning tasks with more challenging work so as to accommodate the specific strengths of high-ability students)

- Built constructive relationships with their students that led to greater challenges, motivation, and personal investment

Planning a range of instructional strategies focusing on in-depth analysis is key to properly matching these strategies with the needs of gifted and high-performing students (Borders, Woodley, & Moore, 2014; VanTassel-Baska & Little, 2011). The findings of one study, designed to explore the characteristics of exceptional teachers of gifted students, suggest that teachers considered highly effective in working with gifted students display a strong preference for abstract themes and concepts, have a passion for their discipline, are open and flexible, and value logical analysis and objectivity (Mills, 2003). Francis Archambault and colleagues (1993) surveyed six thousand general education teachers across the United States and found that few of them made modifications for their gifted students. Those who did indicated they assigned advanced reading, enrichment worksheets, projects, and reports. Another study produced similar results with a different sample of teachers (Westberg & Daoust, 2003). A notable finding was that in classrooms with five or more students identified as gifted, teachers provide significantly more opportunities for challenge, choice, and curriculum modifications to *all* of their students than do those with fewer than five gifted students.

Effective teachers of gifted students actively engage them through a variety of instructional activities and strategies (Matsko & Thomas, 2014; VanTassel-Baska & Little, 2011). These include enrichment (Reis, McCoach, Little, Muller, & Kaniskan, 2011) and curriculum compacting (Pierce et al., 2011). Importantly, effective teachers are able to match the individual's abilities with task difficulty. When the match is optimal, boredom is reduced and students tend to demonstrate higher levels of engagement with the learning process (Csikszentmihalyi, Rathunde, & Whalen, 1993). An international cross-case study reveals that effective teachers of talented learners focus on student engagement through environmental and instructional elements in the classroom, with consideration for authenticity in the learning context. They also pay attention to the interaction of instruction and classroom management (Stronge, Little, & Grant, 2009).

How to Move From Research to Practice

Gifted learners tend to be precocious, intense, creative, conceptually advanced, perfectionistic, and full of complex interests. They prefer to learn about complex topics and interconnections among ideas and to choose the format of their learning products (Kanevsky, 2011). Given these characteristics, they need a learning environment that promotes critical thinking and reasoning ability, encourages divergent thinking and creativity, and fosters inquiry and challenging attitudes toward learning. Thus, teachers of gifted and high-ability learners should take their unique needs and abilities into account. These teachers use a variety of methods, such as acceleration, content modification, and curriculum compacting

in order to provide enriching, differentiated activities that foster students' academic growth (Stronge, 2007).

But how can teachers know what to use and when? To match learning opportunities with learning needs, consider the following five principles (Rogers, 2007).

1. Gifted and talented learners need daily challenges in their specific areas of talent.
2. Teachers should provide regular opportunities for gifted learners to be unique and to work independently in their areas of passion and talent.
3. Teachers should provide various forms of subject- and grade-based acceleration to gifted learners as their education needs require.
4. Teachers should provide opportunities for gifted learners to socialize and to learn with peers of similar ability.
5. For specific curriculum areas, teachers must differentiate instructional delivery in regard to pace, amount of review and practice, and organization.

Gifted learners' strengths need to be identified and supported. These five principles can help provide enriching and challenging learning experiences that stretch and develop students' strengths rather than waste time with the content and skills they have already mastered.

Their social and emotional needs also need to be supported. Gifted students may experience a range of socio-emotional difficulties, such as peer exclusion, isolation, stress, depression, and destructive perfectionism, and these difficulties can lead to gifted underachievement—an incongruence between learning ability and performance (Blaas, 2014). When the gifted students cannot relate to their age-related peers due to advanced cognitive development, teachers can provide opportunities for them to spend time with their true peers who share their interests and abilities.

For more specific guidance in how to differentiate instruction for gifted learners, consider Joyce VanTassel-Baska's (2003) recommendations.

- **Acceleration:** Teachers assign gifted learners fewer tasks to master certain learning standards and cluster learning by higher-order thinking skills.

- **Complexity:** Teachers prompt students to use multiple higher-level skills, add more variables to study, and require multiple resources.
- **Depth:** Teachers have gifted learners study a concept in multiple applications, conduct original research, and develop a product.
- **Challenge:** Teachers use advanced resources and sophisticated content stimuli, employ cross-disciplinary applications, and make the importance of reasoning explicit.
- **Creativity:** Teachers design or construct a model based on principles or criteria; provide alternatives for tasks, products, and assessments; and emphasize oral and written communication to a real-world audience.

For instance, to enhance the complexity of an assignment on the worldwide economic recession, the teacher can introduce the following facets of the issue (VanTassel-Baska, 2014). Question-asking is a deliberate strategy to facilitate thinking of different types and depths. Teachers can use these questions to stimulate student thinking, provide means of thinking, and prompt students to provide clarification of their thinking.

- **Concepts:** What *concepts* allow us to understand the state of the world economy?
- **Purpose:** *Why* do we need to study the state of the economy? What is the economy's role in our lives?
- **Point of view:** What *perspectives* inform our understanding of this crisis? How do economists perceive it? Business people? The general public?
- **Assumptions:** What *assumptions* have countries made about the nature and duration of the recession? What evidence exists to test these assumptions?
- **Data and evidence:** What *evidence* would convince you that the recession is ending? What data sources provide such evidence?
- **Inference:** What *conclusions* can we draw from the evidence about the impact of the recession or depression on a country's well-being? Use your own country as an example.
- **Consequences and implications:** What are the *implications* of worldwide economic stagnation? In the short run? In the long run?

VanTassel-Baska (2011) suggests that teachers make the lessons meaningful and substantive, emphasizing depth over breadth and concept over facts and grounding them in real-world issues and problems that students care about and need to know. It's also important to employ higher-order thinking and reasoning as often as possible through strategies such as concept mapping and persuasive writing. Another way to deepen learning is to use overarching concepts, themes, and issues as organizers, encouraging students to focus on intradisciplinary and interdisciplinary connections. For instance, the themes of change, structure, and beauty are relevant to multiple disciplines such as literature, mathematics, or art. Students should have plenty of opportunities for metacognition, such as planning, monitoring, and assessing their own learning for efficiency and effectiveness. By doing so, they develop habits of mind—curiosity, objectivity, skepticism, and so on—that resemble those of professionals. Similarly, such deeper learning helps students become sensitive to multicultural and global concerns and the importance of multiple perspectives.

Regardless of the approach, teachers should promote inquiry-based learning and problem solving. Creating digital written and visual products or communicating with experts online, for instance, uses technologies to advance the complexity of student learning. Focusing on increasing the significance of learning outcomes (such as making them broad, conceptual, and relevant to real-world applications) and using authentic assessments (such as portfolios and performance-based activities) take these lessons to the next level for gifted students. By employing multiple resources and materials, teachers allow for flexibility, variety, and sophistication in learning.

Susan Johnsen and Gail Ryser (1996) examine 675 articles and 83 abstracts to identify research-based classroom practices for gifted students in the regular classroom. They categorize these effective practices into five domains.

1. **Content:** The way a teacher organizes content, processes, and products to meet student interests and abilities
2. **Rate:** The acceleration or variance of instructional pace
3. **Preference:** A match between a student and a learning style or interest
4. **Environment:** The classroom organization, grouping, and the use of other settings
5. **Instructional strategy:** The methods and pedagogy used in the classroom

This meta-analysis and many later studies (such as Matthews, Ritchotte, & McBee, 2013, and Pierce et al., 2011) find that gifted students benefit from learner-centered learning, open-ended and higher cognitive learning, problem-based learning, accelerated pace of instruction, and clustering with peers of similar learning ability level. Thinking along these five specific elements can help make the practice of differentiation actionable. The core of differentiation is to proactively adjust instruction in tiers to meet students where students are. Similarly, David Sousa and Carol Ann Tomlinson (2011), along with Tomlinson and Marcia Imbeau (2010), also list practices through which to implement differentiation for gifted students.

- **Content:** The knowledge, understanding, and skills that students will learn
- **Process:** Activities through which students make sense of content
- **Product:** How students demonstrate what they know, understand, and can do after learning
- **Affect:** Students' feelings and emotional needs
- **Environment:** Classroom grouping, organization, and management

Regardless of which practices a teacher uses, he or she can differentiate according to student needs and variance. Teachers should consider each student's readiness (proximity to learning goals), interests (proclivities for particular knowledge, understanding, or skills), and learning profile (preferred learning styles or models) when they differentiate a lesson. This list of practices is not significantly different from what is known about differentiation in general education class. Indeed, teachers who are aware of the special needs of their gifted students are naturally driven toward differentiated strategies that help all learners. Rather than just teaching to the middle constantly, they provide targeted content and tasks so that all students can learn at a moderately challenging level. Therefore, differentiated instruction supports not only the efforts of learners with advanced learning ability but also all students.

Summary

James Gallagher (2005) insightfully observed that two predominant values of American education—equity and excellence—have often been in a struggle for scarce education resources. Equity aims for *all* children to learn and acquire needed skills, regardless of their socioeconomic background; and excellence strives for children to achieve as far and as high as they are capable. Because of the urgency and focus on addressing the problems of equity, excellence hasn't been the top priority in education. The responsibility of assessing and recognizing the needs of gifted learners is thus handed to the schools and the classroom teachers. Effective teachers not only educate everyone to meet the basic standard but also help each student fulfill the maximum of his or her learning capacities.

Clearly, individual differences exist in every classroom, and they influence teaching outcomes (Borich, 2011). Differentiated instruction recognizes students' varying needs and variable progress. Teachers who use differentiated instruction maximize each student's potential by accommodating his or her individual strengths and weaknesses and closely aligning the student's readiness with learning outcomes and learning activities. To close the chapter, we include several handouts to help teachers as they effectively integrate differentiation for gifted students into the classroom.

The handout "Differentiation Lesson Plan" (page 23) provides a lesson plan template that helps the teacher think about students' needs and differentiate the learning objectives, learning activities, and assessments so that all students—including gifted learners—can engage with meaningful learning.

We adapted the handout "Self-Assessment Checklist" (page 24) from the work of Arthur Cropley (2001) to help the teacher review his or her own practices in order to evaluate how well he or she fosters development of students' creative thinking, learning, and acting.

Ann Robinson, Bruce Shore, and Donna Enersen (2007) developed an evidence-based guide that identifies and explores twenty-nine research-supported best practices. We discuss the more prominently recommended strategies for differentiating instruction for gifted learners in the handout "Research-Supported Practices in Gifted Education" (page 26). Teachers may find these appropriate for their own teaching and learning situations.

Differentiation Lesson Plan

Teacher:	**Grade Level and Subject:**

Topic:

Standard:

Differentiation based on:

☐ Academic strengths

☐ Student interests and preferences

☐ Special learning needs (remedial or advanced)

Portion of lesson differentiated:

☐ Learning objectives

☐ Content

☐ Instructional strategies (including, but not limited to, curriculum compacting, curriculum extensions, higher-order questioning strategies, advanced-level projects, acting as a practitioner in the field, active learning, higher-order thinking skills, departmentalized teaching, and flexible grouping)

☐ Desired product

☐ Assessment

Self-Assessment Checklist

	Self-Reflection
Component 1: Divergent Thinking	
• Is the teacher open and sensitive to problems students raise? • Does the teacher try to make students aware of open questions, sensitive to their environment, and willing to use all their senses? • Are problems simply presented or, to the maximum degree possible, discovered? • Do time and organization allow for more than one attempt at finding a solution? • Are objects and topics considered from different aspects? • Are students encouraged to not always be satisfied with the first correct solution? • Is a novel method or solution encouraged and appreciated?	
Component 2: General Knowledge and Thinking Base	
• Do learning tasks require and promote broad and differentiated perceptions, or do they restrict variability? • Does learning use different sensory channels and varying methods so that experiences and knowledge may be anchored and accessible in memory storage in various ways? • Is there a focus on the learning process and not simply on the results? • Are *why* questions asked and answered so that cause-effect relationships can be studied? • Is there instruction on systematically analyzing and synthesizing knowledge, themes, issues, topics, facts, problems, and so on? • Do learning challenges require both inductive and deductive reasoning? • Is the learning process made explicit and reflected on with students so that metacognitive thinking is initiated and furthered?	
Component 3: Expansion of Specific Knowledge Base and Specific Skills	
• Is the development of special interests encouraged, for example, by additive or extracurricular provisions, mentor systems, competitions, and so on? • Are sufficient time and resources provided to empower students to conduct independent study and free exploration? • Are individual interests brought into or built into schoolwork?	

	Self-Reflection
Component 4: Focusing and Task Commitment	
<ul><li>Is sustained occupation with a special activity allowed or supported (for example, a project carried on for a semester or the entire school year)?</li><li>Does the planning timetable support such activities?</li><li>Are students assisted to direct their own learning?</li><li>Is there an expectation that tasks have to be fulfilled and brought to an end?</li><li>Are students supported in recognizing and avoiding distractions?</li><li>Are skills of self-monitoring and self-evaluation developed?</li></ul>	
Component 5: Motive and Motivation	
<ul><li>Are students' questions accepted and expanded on?</li><li>Is curiosity stimulated and supported?</li><li>Do students have ownership regarding what they learn and how they learn it?</li><li>Are there opportunities for self-directed learning and discovery learning in order to support and promote intrinsic motivation?</li><li>Are individual interests appreciated and supported?</li><li>Is unnecessary repetition avoided?</li></ul>	
Component 6: Openness and Tolerance of Ambiguity	
<ul><li>Is school not only a place for traditional instruction but also a place of living, of fun, of mental adventure?</li><li>Does instruction bring the real world into school?</li><li>Is there a place for laughter (not at the expense of others) and appreciation of humor?</li><li>Is the teacher able to accept an open result (when appropriate) for an instructional unit?</li><li>Are reasonable risk taking and errors allowed, or are quick and correct results demanded?</li><li>Are the individuality and uniqueness of each student appreciated, or is conformist behavior demanded?</li></ul>	

Source: Adapted from Cropley, A. J. (2001). Creativity in education and learning: A guide for teachers and educators. Philadelphia: Kogan Page.

Research-Supported Practices in Gifted Education

Circle *yes* or *no* for each bolded practice to denote whether it is appropriate for your school or classroom.

Acceleration: This practice involves moving through the traditional curriculum at rates faster than typical.

Appropriate?	Yes	No

Curriculum compacting: This is a strategy to streamline the regular learning scope or sequence for gifted students who can master learning at a faster pace. Teachers can compact learning content into a shorter time period to eliminate the time spent covering the learning objectives that students have already mastered and replace them with more rigorous options.

Appropriate?	Yes	No

Enrichment: This strategy includes approaches that provide deeper and richer learning plans that the typical student cannot necessarily master in the available time.

Appropriate?	Yes	No

Learning centers: These can serve as a focal point for enrichment and acceleration activities.

Appropriate?	Yes	No

Higher-order learning: This practice involves creative and divergent thinking activities and problem-based learning.

Appropriate?	Yes	No

Independent study: This practice involves guided plans for how students can pursue more individualized learning opportunities and lessons.

Appropriate?	Yes	No

Advanced curriculum units: Teachers specifically develop these units for gifted learners. They contain advanced content, high-level process and product work, and intra- and interdisciplinary concept development and understanding.

Appropriate?	Yes	No

Source: Adapted from Robinson, A., Shore, B. M., & Enersen, D. L. (2007). Best practices in gifted education: An evidence-based guide. Waco, TX: Prufrock Press.

Chapter 3
Delivering Differentiated Instruction for Culturally and Linguistically Diverse Students

Throughout its history, the United States has been a magnet for immigration. However, the rate of immigration into the United States from around the world has escalated since the 1970s, meaning that many classrooms have become more diverse communities of learners as each year passes. In 2012, students of color made up more than 45 percent of the preK–12 population, whereas teachers of color made up only 17.5 percent of the educator workforce (Deruy, 2013). Additionally, the numbers of culturally and linguistically diverse students are projected to continue rising. Interestingly, this pattern of increased diversity isn't unique to the United States; Canada, along with many European and Asian countries (such as Sweden and Singapore), has experienced unprecedented rates of immigration since the 1990s (OECD, 2009). The movement of people across the world seems to be continuing unabated.

These changes raise questions about teachers' efficacy in working with students from cultural backgrounds that differ from their own. While an effective teacher will consider the unique learning needs of diverse students when planning and delivering instruction, increasing diversity and changing demographics in school communities complicate this directive. Teachers continue to face challenges in providing appropriate classroom environments and high standards of instruction that foster the academic achievement of all students, particularly minorities and students from low socioeconomic backgrounds (Bloom & Peters, 2012; McAllister & Irvine, 2008). Francisco Hidalgo, Rudolfo Chávez-Chávez, and Jean Ramage (1996) developed a theoretical framework to aid teachers in envisioning an effective, culturally responsive teacher. It involves:

1. Valuing demographic diversity as an enriching social context;
2. Promoting a multicultural curriculum as a whole-school knowledge base;
3. Promoting instructional strategies that structure heterogeneous, learner-centered, and critical processes; and
4. Promoting collaborative and unifying relationships among all participants. (p. 765)

What is culturally responsive instruction? Au (2009) defines it as a "form of teaching that is based on the idea that students of diverse cultural and linguistic backgrounds can be successful in school if lessons and activities build on the strengths they bring from home" (p. 30); furthermore, the purpose of culturally responsive instruction is not "simply to allow children to feel comfortable" but to "improve students' opportunities for academic success by letting their existing strengths and interests serve as a bridge to the new learning offered by the school" (p. 30). Thus, in this chapter, we address how to define, design, and deliver high-quality, responsive learning opportunities in highly diverse classrooms.

What Research Says About Delivering Differentiated Instruction for Culturally and Linguistically Diverse Students

A plethora of studies have examined instructional practices that are effective in culturally and linguistically diverse schools. Research from Megan Bang and Douglas Medin (2010), as well as Eugene Garcia (1991), indicates that classrooms that minority students are academically successful in usually have the following attributes.

- Teachers emphasize functional communication between him- or herself and students and among fellow students.
- Teachers build the instruction of skills and academic content on an understanding of how culture impacts student learning.
- Teachers organize instruction in a way that requires students to interact with each other using collaborative learning techniques.
- Teachers commit to the success of their students and serve as student advocates.

Bang and Medin (2010) also argue that the STEM disciplines (science, technology, engineering, and mathematics) are not acultural, as typically perceived. Rather, they find that instruction that incorporates community-based learning and culture-specific ways of learning or knowing can significantly increase student science learning, and specifically for Native American students in their study. For instance, for the goals of learning about nature, Native American parents said they want their children to realize that they are an integral part of nature, and they are more likely to relate to nature spiritually, while European American parents perceive nature as an externality that needs to be respected and taken care of. The authors find it is important to recognize that science and science education have cultural values, and without such recognition, teachers may implicitly or explicitly exclude students of diversity from their own orientation of the dominant culture. Based on another study (Hughes et al., 2004), achievement and active engagement increase when teachers deliver culturally responsive instruction that connects students' academic work to their cultural characteristics, experiences, and perspectives; use active teaching methods; communicate high expectations; and employ small-group instruction. Students' perceptions of belonging to their school community and their ability to succeed academically also improve (Hughes et al., 2004).

Terrie Epstein, Edwin Mayorga, and Joseph Nelson (2011) find that culturally responsive approaches make the histories and views of marginalized people of color an essential dimension of curriculum. Culturally responsive teaching is an important means to promote the academic achievement and cultural competence of students of color, as well as to facilitate their abilities to critique power relations and, as a class, promote equality and social justice. Specific strategies for culturally responsive teaching include classroom discussion, informative documentaries, simulations, and role playing.

According to Louis Nadelson et al. (2012), "Effective teaching in multicultural settings requires the awareness and ability to adapt to diverse needs and viewpoints" (p. 1183). One effective way for teachers to improve multicultural efficacy is through interactions with diverse communities (Nadelson et al., 2012). Based on their review of research, Gretchen McAllister and Jacqueline Jordan Irvine (2008) suggest that, "in order for teachers to be effective with diverse students, it is crucial that they first recognize and understand their own worldviews; only then will they be able to understand the worldviews of their students" (p. 63). According to Diane Bloom and Terri Peters (2012), "Teachers who demonstrate culturally responsive pedagogy are caring teachers who have high expectations for all students and also provide constructive feedback to students" (p. 73). Additionally, they reflect on their own worldviews and continuously attempt to understand their students (Rychly & Graves, 2012).

How to Move From Research to Practice

Before designing and implementing an instructional program or making instructional modifications for culturally and linguistically diverse students, teachers should consider a pair of key prerequisites: learn about the students and purposefully seek to better understand student diversity.

Learn About the Students

It probably has always been true that learning as much as possible about individual students is essential to planning effective instruction; with diverse students it is doubly important to be sensitive to building culturally responsive instruction, especially regarding current learning proficiency, prior learning experiences, and life experiences. Building new learning activities on students' prior knowledge not only facilitates content learning but also makes the students feel more comfortable and confident in the classroom. Thus, it is essential that teachers consider sources of information concerning students, their families, and community organizations to shed light on instructional planning and delivery (Peregoy & Boyle, 2000). Unless a teacher understands the diversity reflected in his or her students, connecting students' prior knowledge to quality learning experiences becomes extremely challenging.

Understand Cultural Diversity

Teachers should understand cultural diversity and how it impacts teaching, learning and achievement, and assessment. For instance, the directions or items on a test can vary in the amount of language that may be linguistically or culturally demanding, depending on the students' cultural and linguistic backgrounds. Consequently, the test results may underestimate what students from diverse backgrounds know and are able to do. Therefore, effective teachers need to develop a knowledge base about multicultural assessment and other background issues. They need to consider several factors while developing culturally sensitive assessments and interpreting results, including individuals' heritage, religion, history of immigration, family child-rearing practices, language skills, gender roles, views about authority figures, and ways of knowing and seeing (Carjuzaa & Ruff, 2010; Comas-Diaz, 2000). Even at a very basic level, the teacher should know what language is spoken in the student's home and how long the student has been speaking English. When a teacher is highly attentive to these simple markers, it can go a long way toward helping him or her understand the importance of student differences.

Let's use an example to elaborate. In the subject area of history, culturally responsive teaching requires teachers to present issues of race and racism, which connote a complex set of relationships. The concept of racism is pervasive in its effects on economic and political life, as well as social and cultural experiences. Teachers who are culturally responsive integrate into their teaching subtle and individual examples of discrimination or racism, as well as more structural forms of oppression, in efforts to prepare young people of color for their own encounters with and resistance to acts of racism (Epstein et al., 2011). For instance, teachers tend to present Native Americans as victims of settler encroachment only during colonial times and the late nineteenth century and African Americans as victims during slavery and victors during the civil rights movement. Instead of providing this disjointed presentation, teachers who are culturally responsive recognize the inequality in historical and contemporary societies holistically. They also make the histories and views of marginalized people of color an integral part of the curriculum and reframe people of color not just as victims but also agentic actors in history and society. This inclusion challenges students' preconceptions and the stereotypical views of marginalized groups and helps them develop balanced and positive attitudes to diverse ethnic groups.

Once the teacher considers these prerequisite issues, his or her next objective is to design and implement a culturally appropriate instructional program.

Design and Implement Successful Culturally Responsive Instruction

Based on empirical research, a practical guide to differentiating instruction for culturally and linguistically diverse students includes the following components (Cheesman & De Pry, 2010; Garcia, 1991; Gorski, Davis, & Reiter, 2012).

- **High expectations:** Any curriculum, including one for classrooms with high diversity, must be rigorous and address all categories of learning goals (cognitive and academic, advanced as well as basic). Teachers should not lower their expectations for culturally and linguistically diverse students; these students, too, need intellectual challenges.

- **Relevancy:** The more linguistically and culturally diverse the students in a classroom, the more closely the teacher must relate academic content to a student's own environment and experience. The teachers must understand the role of culture in education and throughout society, take responsibility to learn about the particular culture and community, and use the student's culture as a foundation for designing and delivering instruction in a caring manner.

- **Unified curriculum:** The more diverse the students, the more unified the curriculum should be. That is, teachers should center multiple content areas (mathematics, science, social studies) and language learning activities on a single theme. Students should have opportunities to study a topic in depth and to apply a variety of skills acquired in home, community, and school contexts.

- **Meaningfulness:** The more diverse the students, the more important it is to offer them opportunities to apply what they learn in a meaningful context. Teachers can make curriculum meaningful in a number of ways. Students can effectively apply their academic skills, for example, through hands-on, interactive activities that allow them to explore issues of significance in their lives, such as an investigation of issues of race and justice in contemporary society.

- **Learning environment:** It is important to create a learning environment that is respectful of students' cultural heritages, norms, and traditional ways of thinking. Teachers should provide opportunities for students to learn from each other, along with guidance on being comfortable with diversity.

Culturally responsive teachers demonstrate great interest in their students, and they take efforts to know them both as individuals and members of a community. They honor the diversity of belief systems and cultural heritage of the students, and they understand that academic learning is not free of cultural values. They respond to the diversity proactively through adjusting the curriculum, instruction, and classroom management to meet students' cultural, personal, and academic needs (Polleck & Shabdin, 2013; Weinstein, Tomlinson-Clarke, & Curran, 2004). As a result, when students perceive that their teachers are invested in knowing their cultural backgrounds, personal experiences, and interests, they respect the teachers and show higher engagement with learning (Brown-Jeffy & Cooper, 2011).

Summary

The cultural gap between students and teachers has been widening, with students becoming increasingly more diverse and teachers being mostly white, middle-class women. Nowadays, teachers often need to teach students of cultural backgrounds different from their own. Differentiation and cultural sensitivity are becoming an essential part of quality instruction. Differentiating instruction based on students' linguistic and cultural background not only creates a more equitable learning environment but also makes the learning connected to students in a deeper and more meaningful manner. It is important to establish at the very beginning of the school year that the teachers value the presence of the students in the classroom and are eager to get to know them as individuals both academically and personally.

To help teachers effectively differentiate the curriculum for a diverse classroom, we've put together a collection of ready-to-use handouts.

Any good teacher knows that a classroom with just a few students is diverse; after all, no two students are alike. Instruction must be culturally and linguistically fair and bias-free in a classroom of diversity—indeed, any classroom. This means teachers consistently must be culturally conscious with learning materials, tasks, assessments, and classroom interactions. The handout "Teacher Reflection" (page 32) helps teachers be mindful of these issues as they design and deliver high-quality instruction.

Culturally responsive instruction can enhance student academic achievement while still encouraging students to take pride in their own cultural identity. Geneva Gay (2000) provides a useful theoretical framework to describe six main characteristics of culturally responsive instruction. The handout "Culturally Responsive Instruction" (page 33) builds on these six characteristics to help teachers think about how to use culture as a powerful tool that can influence teaching and learning positively.

Culture influences students' approaches to learning and thinking. Although it is important that the teacher never adhere so strongly to generalizations or frameworks of certain ethnic groups that they become stereotypes, it might be helpful to understand students' learning preferences at an individual student level. The purpose of the handout "Student Learning Profile" (page 34) is to provide teachers with a structured way to understand their students' background and learning needs.

Teacher Reflection

	Materials	Tasks	Assessments	Classroom Interactions
Are the views of students of diverse ethnic backgrounds equally and equitably represented?				
Is there any language in the curriculum or instructional materials that is biased, discriminatory, or offensive?				
Is the content respectful and responsive to students of diverse cultures?				
Are diverse culturally responsive learning styles accommodated?				
Does the content reflect high expectations that all students are capable of learning and will succeed in learning?				
Are minority perspectives incorporated into the lesson design and delivery?				

Please use the following questions to reflect on your multicultural efficacy.

	A Great Deal	Much	Somewhat	Little	Never
Are my ideas and opinions of students based on stereotypes or on objective perceptions?					
To what extent do I reach out and interact with people from the community with culturally diverse backgrounds?					
To what extent do I know the customs, traditions, values, and beliefs of the diverse students in my classroom?					
Do I have a genuine acceptance for students regardless of culture, ethnicity, race, and socioeconomic background?					
To what extent do I base learning experiences on the rich diversity and cultural backgrounds of my students?					

Culturally Responsive Instruction

	Strategies I Will Use . . . (This could include service learning, storytelling, creative writing, cooperative learning, community involvement, seminars, discussions, dialogues, and so on.)
Validating	
Acknowledge the legitimacy of the cultural heritage of different ethnic groups, both as legacies that affect students' dispositions, attitudes, and approaches to learning, and as worthy content to be taught in the formal curriculum.	
Build bridges of meaning between home and school experiences, as well as between academic abstractions and lived sociocultural realities.	
Use a wide variety of instructional strategies that match with different learning styles.	
Teach students to know and appreciate their own and others' cultural heritage.	
Incorporate multicultural information, resources, and materials in all subjects and skills routinely taught in the classroom.	
Comprehensive	
Teach the whole child by developing students' intellectual, social, emotional, and political learning; enhance connections to the community to instill collective attitudes of success and commitment.	
Multidimensional	
Encompass curriculum content, learning context, classroom climate, student-teacher relationships, instructional techniques, and performance assessments; explore multiple perspectives; collaborate crossdisciplinarily to teach key themes or issues.	
Empowering	
Help students believe they can succeed in learning tasks and can overcome setbacks to pursue success relentlessly; develop structure and provide resources to boost the probability of student success.	
Transformative	
Develop academic success and cultural consciousness simultaneously; encourage students to give back to their respective communities and participate fully in overall society; help students understand the social structures and processes related to discrimination and prejudice, and develop skills to remove them.	
Emancipatory	
Help students realize that no single version of the truth is total and permanent in all circumstances; give students the freedom to move beyond traditional canons of knowledge to engage in new ways of knowing and thinking, find their own voices, and contextualize issues in multiple cultural perspectives.	

Source: Gay, G. (2000). Culturally responsive teaching: Theory, research, and practice. New York: Teachers College Press.

Student Learning Profile

Student: _____

Cultural background (families, important people, special holidays, and so on):

_____

Learning styles:

- Verbal-Linguistic
- Auditory-Musical
- Visual
- Kinesthetic
- Logical-Mathematical
- Intrapersonal-Solitary
- Interpersonal-Social
- Reflective
- Intuitive
- Sequential
- Global

Learning interests:

_____

Strengths and weaknesses in learning:

_____

I will differentiate the instruction in the following components.

Content:

Process:

Product:

Affect:

Instructional Methods for Differentiation and Deeper Learning © 2016 J. H. Stronge • solution-tree.com
Visit **go.solution-tree.com/instruction** to download this page.

Part II

Deeper Learning Methods for Effective Teaching

The concept of deeper learning has become a vital topic of conversation in U.S. education. The three-part definition of deeper learning given by the American Institutes for Research (2014) has a dual focus on academic learning inside of school and real-world application outside of school:

- A deeper understanding of core academic content
- The ability to apply that understanding to novel problems and situations
- The development of a range of competencies, including people skills and self-control (p. 1)

Given the ever-evolving expectations for education, teachers need to examine how instruction has to adapt to be relevant for students' learning needs for their college, career, and citizenship in the 21st century. What type of teaching can prepare the students to navigate the seismically changing world, have a rewarding career in a rapidly changing workplace, and live a happy and self-fulfilling life? We visualize teaching that develops knowledge, higher-order skills (such as the 4Cs of creativity, critical thinking, communication, and collaboration), and character, as well as establishes lifelong learning habits and an ability to learn how to learn.

In part II, we have selected seven research-based instructional strategies: (1) questioning, (2) metacognition, (3) creativity, (4) critical thinking, (5) complex thinking, (6) active learning, and (7) problem-based learning. These seven chapters will illustrate specific methods to facilitate students' development of a deep understanding of core content and students' ability to think critically, solve problems, communicate effectively, collaborate, self-reflect, and understand how to learn.

Chapter 4

Questioning

Questioning is a technique teachers use to propose a verbal problem to students in order to heighten thinking and learning. Teachers ask questions for a number of purposes, such as getting students' attention, checking and diagnosing students' understanding, structuring and redirecting learning, and keeping students engaged. Questions and answers, from teachers to students and back again, represent much of the interaction that takes place in classrooms.

Questioning can certainly be used ineffectively, so teachers must learn to ask appropriate questions at appropriate times to solicit appropriate information regarding how well students have mastered facts, skills, or ideas in a lesson. Because questioning can encourage student engagement and support a teacher's ability to monitor the learning process and make instructional modifications, an effective teacher would consider his or her instructional repertoire incomplete without a capable command of the skill.

What Research Says About Questioning

Questioning is one of the most widely used instructional practices in education; however, too frequently teachers do not use it to its full advantage. A review of research on teachers' questioning behaviors finds that teachers ask many questions—about fifty questions in a typical class period—but most of the questions are at the lowest cognitive level, known as fact, recall, or knowledge questions (Walsh & Sattes, 2005). One study finds teachers ask about 93 percent of all the questions raised, while students only ask 7 percent (Reinsvold & Cochran, 2012)—revealing the potential for limitations or misuse of questioning as an instructional tool. Furthermore, only 17 percent of teacher questions are open ended, with the majority of those being interpretation questions (versus for application, problem solving, or critical thinking).

Consider the subject area of science; a question such as "Did the temperature go up or down?" is a closed-ended question, since it asks students to make a decision between two options. Questions and prompts like "This is called a what?" or "Plants are producers because . . ." are also closed-ended, as they require students to fill in the blank or complete the definition. The questions "How many categories of rocks have we learned so far?" and "What are the key attributes of sedimentary rock?" are closed-ended as well; they prompt students to determine qualitative or quantitative aspects of a concept.

Let's look at some examples of open-ended questions. For instance, "How would you describe the differences between the igneous rock and the sedimentary rock?" is open-ended, since it focuses on students' interpretations of their observations of two sample rocks. "You made the Coke can roll by using static electricity. What would happen if you add a little water in the can? How much water can it contain until it cannot move? Can you figure out why?" are also open-ended questions that require students to make predictions and provide explanations of the outcomes of an event.

In one study, researchers note that 65 percent of the questions teachers ask are factual and procedural (Vaish, 2013). The questions that elicit extended oral responses from students, such as process and speculative questions, make up only 35 percent of the total. In keeping with this trend, students also ask mainly factual and procedural questions, which make up 73 percent of the total. Only 27 percent of the questions students ask are speculative and process questions. Figure 4.1 summarizes these disconcerting trends in classroom questioning. These findings highlight the importance of not just asking questions but asking the right kinds of questions.

In most cases, not all students are learning at the same level or are expected to have the opportunity to respond to all questions. Teachers frequently call on volunteers, but these volunteers often constitute a select group of students who are very likely to dominate classroom discussion if teachers do not make judicious decisions about assigning the opportunities to their more reticent peers (Walsh & Sattes, 2005). Furthermore, teachers typically wait less than *one second* after asking a question before calling on a student to answer. Walsh and Sattes (2015) find that less than 12 percent of the time, a teacher waits more than three seconds for a response. In addition, teachers wait even less time (virtually no pause) before speaking after a student has answered, which prevents other students from joining the classroom discussion. Teachers also frequently answer their own questions and often accept incomplete or incorrect answers without probing or feedback. When students answer at a cognitive level lower than the teacher questions, teachers generally accept their answers without prompting them to provide better-thought-out responses (Walsh & Sattes, 2015).

Given the concerns about proper use of questioning, here is encouraging news: research indicates that teachers with more subject matter knowledge tend to ask higher-level questions and redirect, prompt, and ask for clarification on student responses more often than do teachers with less subject matter knowledge (Covino & Iwanicki, 1996). We've known this for a long time, but it still holds true: better questioning leads to better learning. And here is another encouraging finding: students with teachers who possess effective questioning skills tend to have better language development and analytical thinking skills than students of teachers who lack questioning skills (Martin, Sexton, & Franklin, 2005).

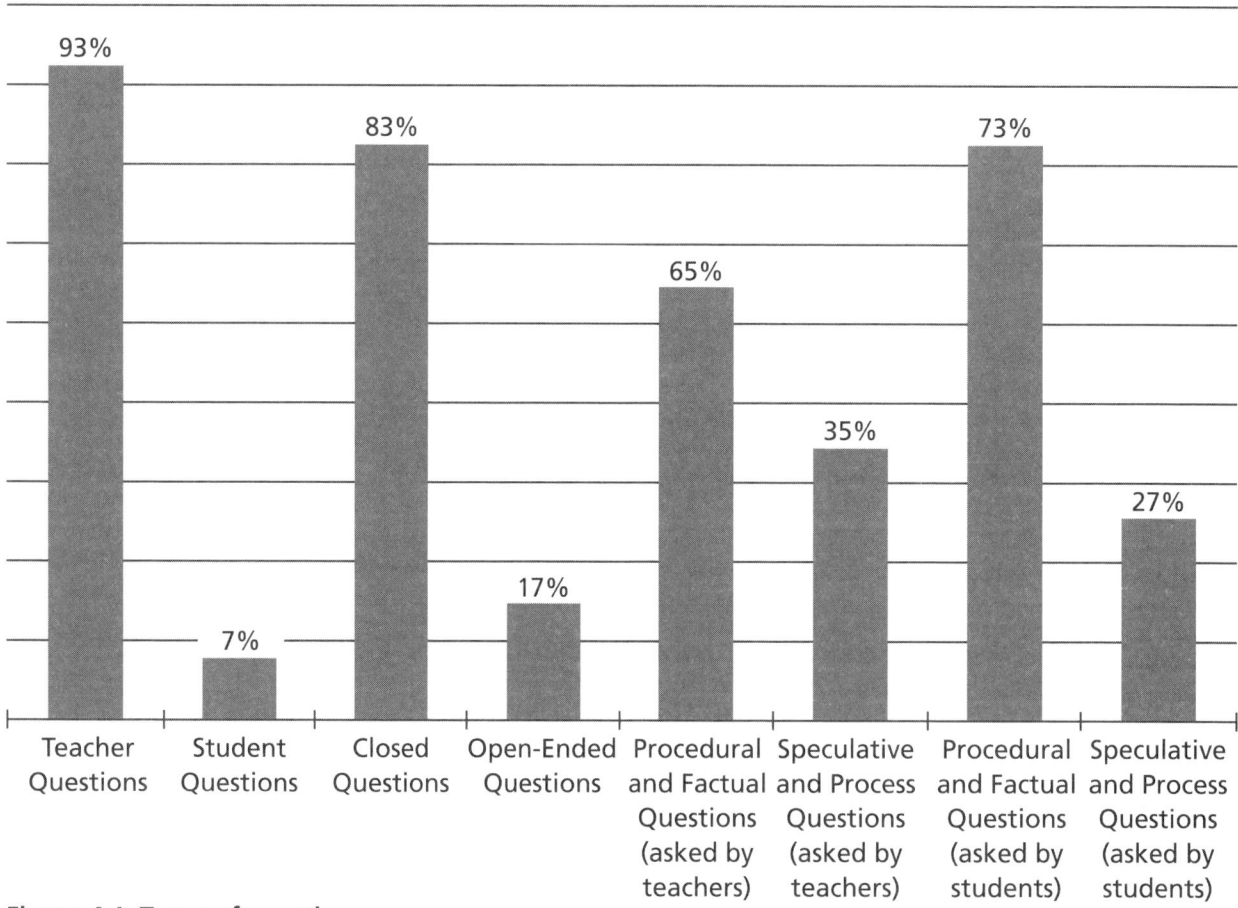

Figure 4.1: Types of questions.

For questioning, more is not always better. Even higher-level questions do not necessarily lead to higher-level responses. Instead, asking content-focused questions that align with learning objectives is the key (Kipper & Rüütmann, 2010). Jackie Walsh and Beth Sattes (2005) identify four characteristics of quality questions.

1. Promote one or more carefully defined instructional purposes.
2. Focus on important content.
3. Facilitate thinking at a stipulated cognitive level.
4. Communicate clearly what the questioner is asking.

Therefore, alignment between questions and learning objectives is the key to quality questioning. Questions that only distract students waste instructional time. Good questions should be able to engage students on the tasks and elicit information about their level of competence on the new learning, and the information can be used to guide teachers' teaching practice.

How to Move From Research to Practice

How do the most effective teachers integrate effective questioning into their daily instructional routines? There is no doubt that good questioning emerges from teaching with an inquiring mind as well as from pure trial and error in practice. However, to expedite the development of good questioning skills, Shy-Jen Guo, Chung-Hsien Tsai, Francis Mou-Te Chang, and Hsu-I Huang (2007) developed a set of guidelines to inform teachers' questioning practices.

- Teachers may prepare questions before class but should remain flexible and adapt to students' reactions in the classroom.
- Teachers should decide which type of question meets the instructional objective.
- Teachers should take into account the learning ability of students.
- Teachers should design questions to create an atmosphere in which all students feel they have the opportunity to participate and that motivates them to actively take part in the discussion (as opposed to singling out students or allowing one student to compete against another).

There are three teacher questioning behaviors in particular that have proven helpful in enhancing student learning: (1) openness, (2) wait time, and (3) feedback.

Openness

Allowing students to answer questions from various points of view may encourage them to actively join the discussions. Teachers should provide neutral rather than evaluative feedback to student responses. Instead of judging the correctness of their responses or giving the correct answer immediately, the teachers can facilitate an in-depth interactive discussion by encouraging students to elaborate on their answers and by prompting them to self-evaluate the answers. Giving students hints and comments, and clarifying students' answers at appropriate moments, can help students reach more accurate or higher-level responses (Guo et al., 2007). Teachers should also maintain flexibility by adjusting questions based on student responses so as to tailor higher-order thinking.

Wait Time

Wait time is an important aspect of questioning; longer wait times relate to higher student achievement, increased participation, and better student-to-student interaction (Cotton, 1989; Stahl, 1994; Tobin, 1980; Tobin & Capie, 1982). Research has associated longer wait times with longer responses, greater numbers of voluntary responses, greater behavioral complexity of the responses, greater frequency of student questions, and increased confidence in responding (Borich, 1988). Overall, research indicates that if teachers increase their average wait time for student response, significant advantages follow: lengthened responses by slow learners, increased creative and complete answers, stronger student confidence, and enhanced student achievement (Guo et al., 2007). Therefore, teachers should not rush the questioning process. Instead, an effective teacher gives students sufficient time to think about the question, formulate their answers, and respond—particularly for higher-level questions.

Feedback

Students need specific feedback during their responses to stimulate further thinking, clarify what is expected of them, correct their errors, and improve their performances. Thus, teachers should use good listening strategies and pay attention to what students say. Appropriate praising or nodding to the responding student with a friendly manner may encourage him or her. In fact, questions are most valuable when they receive responses—correct or incorrect—because responses encourage student engagement, demonstrate understanding or misconceptions, and further the discussion (Brophy & Good, 1986; Cawelti, 2004).

Purposes, Types, and Levels of Questioning

Obviously, teachers intend questions to promote different learning outcomes and to invoke different learning purposes. Because of this, teachers must also recognize what question to use when, and how to mix and match the cognitive complexity of questions.

Table 4.1 provides examples for questions in different instructional situations.

Aside from the various purposes of questions, there are several types of questions that a teacher can choose from, depending on what he or she wants to accomplish through questioning. Table 4.2 (page 42) details questions based on expected answers, learning objectives, and critical thinking, as presented in Guo et al. (2007).

Questioning can also range from lower-level thinking, such as recalling specific facts, to higher-level thinking, such as analyzing or problem solving. It's helpful to consider the proper mix of cognitive complexity in questioning. So, what types of questions do effective teachers ask (Stronge et al., 2007; Taylor, Pearson, Clark, & Walpole, 1999)?

- **Most-effective teachers:** A combination of higher-level questions and lower-level questions
- **Less-effective teachers:** Lower-level and text-based questions

Bloom's revised cognitive taxonomy of learning objectives provides a useful way to think about when and how to use questions (Anderson & Krathwohl, 2001). The framework provides seven major categories in the cognition domain: (1) knowledge, (2) comprehension, (3) application, (4) analysis, (5) synthesis, (6) evaluation, and (7) creation. The categories are ordered from simple to complex and from concrete to abstract. Teachers combine questions that require lower-order thinking (often closed or convergent questions to assess students' knowledge, comprehension, and application) with questions that require higher-order thinking (often open or divergent questions to promote students' skills in analysis, synthesis, evaluation, and creation). For example, the students not only need to be exposed to questions of *why*, *how*, and *when* to recall the facts about the three branches of government, but they also need deeper questions that can probe them to develop understanding about or explain the ideas about democracy, and apply relevant concepts to analyze current real-world problems, or even evaluate societal phenomena.

Summary

Questioning is a valuable instructional tool that serves many purposes: motivating and engaging student attention, evaluating student learning, developing student thinking skills, engaging students in thoughtful discourses, and stimulating students to carry on with inquiry and investigation (Vogler, 2008). Good questions help teachers keep the focus on students and their interactions with the content and with each other rather than focusing on just the content. For quality questioning, teachers understand that they are not the experts who hold the authority over the subject matter; instead, they are facilitators who establish a platform of cognitive engagement for students to construct personal understanding of the content.

We've compiled the following handouts to help teachers phrase the right kinds of questions at the right levels to engage students in everything from basic recall to creation of an idea, based on the intended learning outcomes.

One way to improve teachers' abilities in questioning is for administrators or peers to observe and collect evidence of their questioning behavior. Observers can use the "Questioning Technique Analysis" handout (page 44) as an instrument to accurately record teachers' verbal questioning in the classroom. Then they can use the data they collect as a baseline. After a certain period of time, they conduct

Table 4.1: Questions for Different Purposes

Purpose	Questions
To assess learning	• What is the most important idea that we have covered in today's lesson? • Can you explain the concept in your own words? • Can you draw a diagram to illustrate this idea?
To ask a student to clarify a vague comment	• Can you elaborate on that point? • Can you explain what you mean?
To prompt students to explore attitudes, values, or feelings (when appropriate)	• What are the values or beliefs that inform this argument? • What is your initial reaction to this argument?
To prompt students to see a concept from another perspective	• How do you think those who disagree with you view this issue? • How does that concept apply to this new problem?
To prompt students to support their assertions and interpretations	• How do you know that? • What part of the text led you to that conclusion?
To direct students to respond to one another	• What do you think about the ideas your classmate just presented? • Do you agree or do you see the issue differently? Please explain. • Can you think of another way to solve that problem?
To prompt students to investigate a thought process	• What are the assumptions that informed the design of this experiment? • What are the assumptions that these two arguments share?
To ask students to predict possible outcomes	• What is your prediction of what is going to happen in this story or experiment? • What changes do you want to make to your predictions given the information you already have? • What would happen differently if . . . ?
To prompt students to connect and organize information	• How does the content we learned in this lesson shed light on the concept we studied last week? • Can you develop a graph that organizes this information in a helpful way?
To ask students to apply a principle or formula	• How does this principle apply to the following situation? • Who can suggest how we might use this new formula to solve the problems we examined at the start of class? • Under what conditions is this equation not valid?
To ask students to illustrate a concept with an example	• Can you think of an example of this phenomenon? • Can you point us to a specific part of the text that led you to that conclusion? • Can you identify a painting or design that exemplifies that idea?

Source: Adapted from the Teaching Center, Washington University in St. Louis, 2009.

another observation to assess whether the teacher has made expected improvement in questioning skills.

After thinking about typical practices in classroom questioning, teachers can apply the "Good Questioning Practices Checklist" (page 45) to instructional questioning. Alternatively, the checklist is useful in peer coaching and peer review. We intend for this handout to allow teachers to conscientiously consider effective practices in their everyday use of classroom questioning.

As mentioned earlier in the text, Bloom's taxonomy of learning objectives provides a useful framework for thinking about questioning (Anderson & Krathwohl, 2001). The handout "Questioning for the Learning Domains" (page 46) can help teachers phrase questions at the right levels to engage students.

Table 4.2: Types of Questions

Context	Type of Question
Based on the nature of expected answers	Closed questions (also known as convergent questions), which guide students' thinking to a specific answer based on the materials Purpose: To understand students' learning progress or to remind them to pay attention in the classroom
	Open questions (also known as divergent questions), which have a broad range of acceptable answers, and the answers need only obey basic principles and meet logical inferences Purpose: To stimulate students to deepen and broaden their thinking
Based on learning objectives	Knowledge questions Purpose: To stimulate students to recall, describe, recognize, or define the knowledge or information that they have learned and remembered but not necessarily understood
	Comprehension questions Purpose: To prompt students to understand, explain, summarize, or elaborate the facts, ideas, and principles, and discover the relationship between two or more learning events, such as the ability to understand basic definitions, make comparisons, and draw conclusions about general principles
	Application questions Purpose: To encourage students to apply just-learned knowledge to resolve new problems
	Analysis questions Purpose: To prompt students to break information into components and infer the relationship among them
	Synthesis questions Purpose: To encourage students to integrate what they have learned into a single creative response in either an oral or substantive form
	Evaluation questions Purpose: To encourage students to judge the value of materials (such as statement, novel, poem, research project) through certain criteria which are given them or determined by themselves
Based on ways of critical thinking	Eleven subcategories: 1. Classifying 2. Assuming 3. Predicting (or hypothesizing) 4. Inferring, interpreting data, or making conclusions 5. Measuring 6. Designing an investigation to solve a problem 7. Observing 8. Graphing 9. Reducing experimental error 10. Evaluating 11. Analyzing

Source: Guo et al., 2007.

Students may be reluctant to ask questions in the classroom for many reasons, such as peer pressure and power dynamics with the teacher. When the teacher is the one who constructs the most interesting questions, problems, or challenges, students become dependent on the teacher for initiatives of inquiry. It is just as important to teach students to ask questions as answer them. Teachers can encourage students to develop questions by creating a question-friendly classroom environment. In addition, like asking their own questions, teachers can encourage students to ask higher-order questions like *why* and *how*. In many cases, students find it helpful to have question starter templates available as a framework to fall back on. The handout "Student-Developed Questioning" (page 48) provides types of Socratic questions that teachers can share with students (Intel Teach Program, 2007; University of Michigan, n.d.).

Use the "Content-Focused Questions Design Form" (page 49) to identify the major learning objectives students aim to accomplish and the cognitive levels of learning that they engage in for each objective. Then draft the questions to ask, and check to make sure they align with the cognitive levels and learning content. This is an especially useful tool for building guiding questions into lesson planning.

Questioning Technique Analysis

Directions: Record all the questions the teacher asks orally and in writing during the lesson. Place the question in the space beneath the appropriate level. Then tally the number of questions by level and calculate a percentage.

Teacher's Name: _____ Date: _____

Time Started and Ended: _____

Observer's Name: _____ Grade and Subject: _____

Type of Question	Total #	Percent
Low cognitive (recall)		
Intermediate cognitive (comprehension)		
Application and high cognitive (analysis, synthesis, evaluation)		
Total of all questions		

Based on the percentages, what level of thinking did these questions target?

How clearly worded were the questions?

Instructional Methods for Differentiation and Deeper Learning © 2016 J. H. Stronge • solution-tree.com

Visit **go.solution-tree.com/instruction** to download this page.

Good Questioning Practices Checklist

Did I direct questions to all students?	Yes	No
Did I move the questioning around when calling on students to involve all of them?	Yes	No
Did I provide appropriate wait time before calling on students?	Yes	No
Did I give an appropriate pause before commenting on student responses or before moving on?	Yes	No
Did I use the right balance of lower-cognitive-level questions and higher-order, challenging questions?	Yes	No
Did I encourage students to ask questions of me?	Yes	No
Did I encourage students to ask questions of one another?	Yes	No
Did I teach students how to develop quality questions and questioning strategies?	Yes	No
Did I answer my own questions?	Yes	No

Questioning for the Learning Domains

Cognitive Level	Explanation	Demonstrated By	Prompts
Remembering (Lower)	Recalling previously learned information	arrange, define, describe, duplicate, identify, label, list, match, memorize, name, order, recall, recognize, relate, repeat, select, state	• Who? • Where? • Which one? • What? • How? • Why? • How much? • How many? • When?
Understanding (Lower)	Demonstrating an understanding of facts; explaining ideas or concepts	classify, convert, defend, discuss, distinguish, estimate, explain, give examples, identify, locate, paraphrase, predict, summarize	• What does this mean? • Which are the facts? • State in your own words. • Give an example. • Select the best definition. • Explain why . . . • What expectations are there? • What are they saying? • What's the main idea? • This represents . . .
Applying (Lower)	Using information in another familiar fashion	change, choose, compute, demonstrate, employ, illustrate, interpret, manipulate, modify, practice, prepare, show, sketch, solve, use	• Judge the effects of . . . • What would result . . . ? • Tell what would happen if . . . • Tell how much change there would be if . . . • Identify the results of . . . • How would you solve . . . using what you have learned? • What examples can you provide . . . ? • What facts can you select to support . . . ?

Instructional Methods for Differentiation and Deeper Learning © 2016 Solution Tree Press • solution-tree.com
Visit **go.solution-tree.com/instruction** to download this page.

Cognitive Level	Explanation	Demonstrated By	Prompts
Analyzing (Higher)	Breaking information into parts to explore understandings and relationships	appraise, breakdown, calculate, categorize, compare, contrast, diagram, differentiate, distinguish, examine, infer, model, question, test	• What assumptions . . . ? • What statement is relevant? • What motive is there? • What does the author believe? • What does the author assume? • State the point of view of . . . • What ideas apply? • What's the relationship between . . . ? • The least essential statements are . . . • How could you explain the fact that . . . ? • What is the importance of . . . ?
Evaluating (Higher)	Justifying a decision or course of action; judging based on given criteria; making decisions	appraise, argue, assess, attach, choose, conclude, defend, discriminate, estimate, judge, justify, interpret, rate, support, value	• What fallacies, consistencies, or inconsistencies appear? • Which is more important, moral, better, logical, valid, or appropriate? • Is there a better solution to . . . ? • Judge the value of . . . • What do you think about . . . ? • Can you defend your position about . . . ? • Do you think . . . is a good or bad thing? • How would you have handled . . . ? • What changes to . . . would you recommend?
Creating (Higher)	Generating new ideas, products, or ways of viewing things	assemble, combine, compose, construct, design, develop, devise, formulate, generate, plan, set up, synthesize, tell, write	• Can you design a . . . to . . . ? • Can you see a possible solution to . . . ? • If you had access to all resources, how would you deal with . . . ? • Why don't you devise your own way to . . . ? • What would happen if . . . ? • How many ways can you . . . ? • Can you create new and unusual uses for . . . ? • Can you develop a proposal which would . . . ?

Source: Adapted from Anderson, L. W., & Krathwohl, D. R. (Eds.). (2001). A taxonomy for learning, teaching, and assessing: A revision of Bloom's taxonomy of educational objectives (Complete ed.). New York: Longman.

Student-Developed Questioning

Types of Questions	Sentence Stems
Questions for clarification	• Why do you say that? • What do you mean by . . . ? • Would you put that another way? • Could you give an example? • Could you explain?
Questions that probe assumptions	• What could we assume instead? • How can you verify or disprove that assumption? • You seem to be assuming . . . . Do I understand you correctly?
Questions that probe reasons and evidence	• What would be an example? • What do you think causes . . . to happen? Why? • What information do we need in order to prove . . . ? • What reasoning led you to that conclusion? • What is some evidence that can support your argument?
Questions about viewpoints and perspective	• What would be an alternative? • What is another way to look at it? • Would you explain why it is necessary or beneficial, and who benefits? • Why is this option the best? What are the justifications? • What are the strengths and weaknesses of . . . ? • How are . . . and . . . similar? • What is a counterargument for . . . ? • How would other groups of people respond to this question? Why? • How are the ideas of . . . and . . . alike? Different?
Questions that probe origins or sources	• Is this your idea, or did you hear of it from someplace else? • Has something or someone influenced your opinion? • What caused you to feel that way?
Questions that probe implications and consequences	• What generalizations can you make? • What are the consequences of that assumption? • What are you implying? • How does . . . affect . . . ? • If that happened, what else would happen as a result? Why?
Questions about initial questions or issues	• What was the point of this question? • How does this relate to our discussion? • How does . . . apply to real life? • Why is this question important?

Source: Adapted from Intel Teach Program. (2007). Designing effective projects: Questioning—The Socratic questioning technique. *Accessed at www.intel.com/content/dam/www/program/education/us/en/documents/project-design/strategies/dep-question-socratic.pdf on September 17, 2014; University of Michigan. (n.d.).* The six types of Socratic questions. *Accessed at www.umich.edu/~elements/probsolv/strategy/cthinking.htm on September 17, 2014.*

Content-Focused Questions Design Form

Learning Objective 1:	Appropriate Cognitive Levels: ☐ Knowledge ☐ Comprehension ☐ Application ☐ Analysis ☐ Synthesis ☐ Evaluation ☐ Creation	Sample Questions: ☐ The sample questions align well with the cognitive levels and learning content.
Learning Objective 2:	Appropriate Cognitive Levels: ☐ Knowledge ☐ Comprehension ☐ Application ☐ Analysis ☐ Synthesis ☐ Evaluation ☐ Creation	Sample Questions: ☐ The sample questions align well with the cognitive levels and learning content.
Learning Objective 3:	Appropriate Cognitive Levels: ☐ Knowledge ☐ Comprehension ☐ Application ☐ Analysis ☐ Synthesis ☐ Evaluation ☐ Creation	Sample Questions: ☐ The sample questions align well with the cognitive levels and learning content.

Instructional Methods for Differentiation and Deeper Learning © 2016 J. H. Stronge • solution-tree.com
Visit **go.solution-tree.com/instruction** to download this page.

Chapter 5

Metacognition

In today's world, learning discrete sets of knowledge and skills, as well as mastering their use, is important. However, this isn't enough. Given the dramatic changes that adults have experienced and the accelerating rate of change that students will encounter in their personal lives, teachers must equip students for changing contexts, knowledge and skill sets, and careers.

Indeed, the world is rapidly evolving and ever competitive. What becomes essential, then, is that teachers prepare students to understand and embrace change. Learning is essential but no longer sufficient; what they need is the capacity to *learn how to learn*. In other words, students need to develop a clear, deep mastery of metacognition.

The Greek prefix *meta-* means *beyond*, thus *metacognition* refers to *beyond learning*. As Gregory Thomas (2003) defines it, "Metacognition refers to an individual's knowledge, awareness and control of his/her thinking and learning strategies" (p. 175). Put another way, metacognition is the awareness a person has of the type of cognitive procedures he or she uses in specific instances (Zohar & Peled, 2008). Metacognition—"cognition about cognition" or "knowing about knowing"—can take various forms: "It includes knowledge about when and how to use particular strategies for learning or for problem solving" (Metacognition, n.d.). As Hope Hartman (2001) argues:

> Teachers should not be satisfied with putting students in situations which require them to use [any strategy] (or any strategy they want students to use). Practice isn't enough. It is also important to provide explicit instruction in when, why and how to use [the strategy]; students need to understand the rationale and effective procedures for [the strategy] so that they can recognize appropriate contexts for its use, so that they have criteria for evaluating [their strategy], and so they can self-regulate its use. (p. 56)

Metacognition is a form of self-awareness of learning. It is a higher-order form of thinking that embodies conscious planning, examination, and control of the cognitive processes used in learning.

What Research Says About Metacognition

Research has found that explicit intervention from the teacher can improve students' metacognitive skills. For instance, studies reveal that instruction and metacognitive strategies have a positive impact on student learning in reading (Dabarera, Renandya, & Zhang, 2014), science (Zohar & Barzilai, 2013), and mathematics (Lee, Yeo, & Hong, 2014). In reading, researchers see the most remarkable changes in students' use of metacognitive strategies, such as "I decide in advance to look at the text to see its layout, illustrations, and so on" (with a pretest mean of 3.15 versus a post-test mean of 4.60 out of 5), and "I decide in advance what my reading purpose is, and then I read with that goal in mind" (with a pretest mean of 3.67 versus a post-test mean of 4.42) (Aghaie & Zhang, 2012). Helen Askell-Williams, Michael Lawson, and Grace Skrzypiec (2012) surveyed the status of students' metacognitive knowledge and find it is generally at a less than optimal level with substantial room for improvement. However, this study also finds that when teachers embed explicit cognitive and metacognitive strategic instruction into regular lessons, students' acquisition of strategy knowledge improves.

Anat Zohar and Bracha Peled (2008) assess the effects of explicit teaching of *metastrategic* knowledge on gains of low-achieving and high-achieving fifth-grade students. Gains in reasoning scores of students from the metastrategic knowledge group were statistically significantly higher when compared to students from the control group. These gains were preserved in transfer tasks immediately after the end of instruction and three months later. Explicit teaching of metastrategic knowledge affected both low-achieving and high-achieving students, but it was extremely valuable for low-achieving students, who required a longer period than high-achieving students to reach their top score.

In another study, which examines fourth-grade science reading and task performance, the students who received metacognitive training performed better than students in the control group on all measured outcomes: domain-specific scientific knowledge (about animals and plants in this case), scientific literacy, and metacognitive awareness (Michalsky, Mevarech, & Haibi, 2009). More specifically, those who received metacognitive instruction after the reading significantly outperformed students from the other two groups who received metacognitive intervention before and during reading on all outcome measures. This study suggests that merely exposing students to learning opportunities is insufficient and that explicit instruction in metacognition can train them to self-regulate their learning and achieve better results.

A positive impact from metacognitive instruction is also found in mathematics. One study investigates the differential effects of cooperative learning with or without metacognitive instruction on low and high achievers' solutions for eleventh-grade authentic tasks in mathematics (Kramarski, Mevarech, & Arami, 2002). Results indicate that students who receive metacognitive instruction within cooperative learning significantly outperform their counterparts who experience cooperative learning with no metacognitive instruction.

Collectively, these studies on the impact of metacognitive teaching and learning are impressive. Should we continue to teach students traditional content and skills? Definitely, yes, because they continue to be the basic building blocks for learning. Is this enough? Absolutely not! Teaching how to learn is not a luxury; it is a requirement.

How to Move From Research to Practice

It seems clear that the ability to understand metacognitive thinking and adeptly use its components are essential skills for all of our students. Metacognitive knowledge can be either implicit or explicit (Zohar & Peled, 2008). All learners tend to have general knowledge about their cognitive processes or abilities, such as analyzing causal relationships, constructing good arguments, formulating research questions, testing hypotheses, analyzing and synthesizing information, drawing conclusions, and evaluating. They manipulate and modify these processes, even if unconsciously. However, such knowledge and control can also be publicly and explicitly taught, discussed, and demonstrated in class. In fact, in order to effectively teach learning how to learn—or learning how to think about learning—teachers should overtly discuss and develop metacognitive thinking in classrooms. Specific aspects of metacognitive skill development include the following (Zohar & Peled, 2008).

- Making generalizations and setting rules regarding a thinking strategy
- Naming the thinking strategy
- Explaining when, why, and how one should use the given thinking strategy
- Deciding when one should not use the thinking strategy
- Evaluating disadvantages of not using appropriate strategies
- Deciding what situations or tasks call for the use of the given strategy

To begin developing metacognition skills with students, it is important for teachers to encourage them to ask themselves metacognitive questions that can guide them to be conscious of, monitor, and evaluate the learning process. Given that individual students' construction of knowledge is an internal cognitive operation, teachers can train students to self-regulate their learning processes by prompting them to formulate and answer metacognitive questions that focus on those processes.

Researchers originally designed the following sequence for addressing metacognitive questions for mathematics students (Kramarski et al., 2002; Mevarech & Kramarski, 1997), but others find it equally effective when transferred to other subject areas, such as science (Michalsky et al., 2009).

1. **Comprehend the problem:** What is the problem all about? Why does the problem need investigation?

2. **Build connections between previous and new knowledge:** What do you already know about the problem? What are the similarities and differences between the problem at hand and the problems you have encountered in the past? Please explain your reasoning.

3. **Use strategies appropriate for solving the problem:** What inquiry strategies, tactics, or principles are appropriate for solving the problem? When and how should you implement a particular strategy? Please explain your reasoning.

4. **Reflect on the thinking processes and the solution:** Does the solution make sense? Can you design the processes in another way? How? Please explain your reasoning.

This sequence can be used for development of metacognition in various age groups and content areas. Particularly, this sequence works best in cooperative learning settings and for the subject of mathematics, in which students work in small groups to reason mathematically by formulating and answering a series of self-addressed metacognitive questions (Kramarski et al., 2002).

Providing students with support as they develop metacognitive strategies is essential for them to feel comfortable with these strategies and their benefits (Thomas, 2003). Robert Sternberg (1998) notes that students may not be enthusiastic about developing metacognition, especially when they "have been rewarded over the years for passive and rather mindless learning" (as cited in Thomas, 2003, p. 129). Students need consistent support to engage in metacognitive thinking because of their inexperience and reluctance. A supportive learning environment for metacognitive skill development might include the following aspects (Thomas, 2003).

- **Metacognitive demands:** Teachers ask students to be aware of how they learn and how they can improve their learning.
- **Teacher modeling and explanation:** Teachers model and explain learning processes to students.
- **Student-student discourse:** Students discuss their learning processes with each other.
- **Student-teacher discourse:** Students discuss their learning processes with their teacher.
- **Student voice:** Students feel it is legitimate to question the teacher's pedagogical plans and methods.
- **Distributed control:** Students collaborate with the teacher to plan their learning while they develop as autonomous learners.
- **Teacher encouragement and support:** Teachers encourage students to improve their learning processes.
- **Emotional support:** Teachers care for students emotionally in relation to their learning.

Let's use an eighth-grade language arts lesson plan as an example to demonstrate how a teacher could enhance his or her students' metacognitive thinking as they read a text (figure 5.1, page 54).

The teacher reflects on the lesson plan as follows:

> This lesson is a continuation of lessons focused on talking to the text. We know that good readers actively interact with text in many ways. This lesson continues to reinforce and explicitly show students what effective readers do when they are reading. I know that direct instruction is critical in many lessons. I also realize that students need an opportunity to practice what I have taught while receiving feedback. This is where guided practice comes in. Additionally, I want students to share their thoughts with others so that they can clarify, expand, and refine their thinking. One way to do that is with conversations with others. I know that there is an artificiality to this lesson in that most often we read independently and don't interact by writing down what we think about. However, until this becomes ingrained

Common Core State Standards Addressed

RL.7.1: Cite several pieces of textual evidence to support analysis of what the text says explicitly as well as inferences drawn from the text.

RL.7.2: Determine a theme or central idea of a text and analyze its development over the course of the text; provide an objective summary of the text.

RL.7.3: Analyze how particular elements of a story or drama interact (e.g., how setting shapes the characters or plot).

RL.7.6: Analyze how an author develops and contrasts the points of view of different characters or narrators in a text.

Introduce Learning Objectives

Students will be able to read aloud and analyze text through use of double-entry journals in small groups.

Students will be able to "talk" to the text (make inferences, draw conclusions, question the text, and generate higher-level thoughts).

Procedures

1. Do Now Activity: Make a list of three to five detailed predictions about the book *Rikki-Tikki-Tavi* through reading, using title, headings, bold words, and pictures in the textbook. Students will share their predictions with the class.

2. Introduction to Today's Lesson: Use a double-entry journal format to talk to the text. (Students have been using sticky notes to do this over the past week. We are continuing with these good reading strategies in a different format.) Discuss what I expect to see in the journal entry—opinions, thoughts, predictions, comparing and contrasting, connections, inferences, and conclusions—and what I don't expect to see—summaries.

3. Guided Practice: Students and teacher work together on the first two entries to ensure understanding of how and what to do. Explain and demonstrate what talking to the text means—comparing and contrasting, making connections, understanding important clues, and drawing inferences about what is unsaid based on what is actually said in the text.

4. Independent Practice: Students work together to talk to the text. Then each of the groups shares its "highest level" inference with the rest of the class.

5. Check for Understanding: I will check on groups by reviewing their work and asking questions to ascertain their understanding.

Closure

Teacher and students recap the lesson and review the homework assignment.

Assessment

Formative: The teacher assesses student understanding through anecdotal notes from observation and questions.

Summative: There will be a quiz on the story at the end of the week.

Homework

1. Make a list of characters we have been introduced to so far. Generate a list of character traits about these characters.

2. Write a few sentences describing the setting.

Source: Adapted from NGA & CCSSO, 2010a.

Figure 5.1: Sample eighth-grade language arts lesson with metacognitive thinking.

> and seamless, it's important to practice these reading strategies until they become transparent and are done without thinking. At this point in the reading instruction, I am trying to get students to think metacognitively about reading. I will begin with reading groups in the next two weeks. Presently, we are developing the procedures I want them to use in their groups as a whole class.

All learners are inclined to engage in metacognitive thinking during learning, especially when confronted with demanding and challenging tasks. However, some students have greater metacognitive abilities than the others, and they are more likely to be successful with learning. Teachers can correct this inequity by teaching and enhancing students' repertoire of metacognitive skills. To do this, the teachers model the skills in action (such as through think-alouds, demonstrating how to use organizers, and modeling thought processes in solving problems) and prompt students to employ the practices to monitoring their learning.

Summary

Metacognition emphasizes the importance of the role of elaboration in constructing new learning. Students with metacognitive skills can supply explanations, expound on their reasoning, and monitor their learning process. They also know what tool to use for completing tasks, modifying learning strategies when needed, identifying obstacles in learning, and overcoming the challenges for goal attainment. Teachers should teach metacognitive skills and use them as a lever to improve student learning.

Metacognition involves students actively planning, monitoring, and evaluating knowledge as they learn it. It is a process of tracking progress toward goals. To help teachers incorporate metacognition into the classroom, we've put together the following collection of handouts.

Teachers can provide the handout "Encouraging Students to Think About Thinking" (page 56) to students or use it as a guideline to identify or generate an effective strategy to tackle a task, monitor problem solving, assess the need for modifications, and measure the success of learning.

Metacognition also involves self-assessment and reflective thinking. One way to develop students' metacognitive skills is to teach them how to ask themselves questions. Thus, the handout "Encouraging Students to Ask Metacognitive Questions" (page 57) provides a list of sample questions that students can use.

In many cases, metacognitive thinking does not come naturally. That is why teachers need to develop and sometimes model metacognition consciously in their classrooms. We designed the handout "Teacher Self-Assessment of Metacognition Use" (page 58) for teachers to reflect on the degree to which their classroom practice promotes students' awareness of their own thinking.

Encouraging Students to Think About Thinking

Planning (Please identify the problem, choose the strategies, and determine if you have the resources to support accomplishment of the task):

Monitoring (Please describe how you will monitor your comprehension and task performance, and please describe the changes you made to the strategies and the justifications for those changes):

Evaluating (Please describe how you will appraise the final product against specific criteria and the effectiveness of the strategies that you used):

Encouraging Students to Ask Metacognitive Questions

- Do I know what the problem is about?

- How much time do I need to set aside to learn this?

- What prior knowledge have I learned that could help me with this task?

- What should I do first?

- What is the action plan?

- Do I understand what I am reading or hearing?

- How could I know if I am on the right track to solve the problem?

- Do I need to move in a different direction?

- Am I making my points clear and understandable?

- How am I doing?

- What can I do differently?

- What additional information do I need?

- Where can I seek the assistance that I need?

- How do the outcomes measure against the criteria of effectiveness and efficiency?

- Does this solution make sense?

- Have I convinced the audience?

- What could I do differently if I have an opportunity to do this again?

- How did this line of thinking help me solve the problem?

- How could I apply this learning and thinking to other problems?

Instructional Methods for Differentiation and Deeper Learning © 2016 J. H. Stronge • solution-tree.com
Visit **go.solution-tree.com/instruction** to download this page.

Teacher Self-Assessment of Metacognition Use

1. What strategies do you use to teach about thinking strategies in your classroom?

2. What kinds of metacognitive strategies are most important in your subject matter? Some examples of metacognitive strategies include planning and organizing, monitoring, and redirecting learning.

3. How do you teach students about these strategies (*what*, *when*, and *how* of the strategies)? Do you embed metacognitive instruction in the content?

4. What kinds of questions do students need to ask themselves to tackle the tasks in your subject matter?

5. Do your students have an awareness of knowledge? Do they understand what they already know, what they do not know, and what they want to know?

6. Do your students always understand when and why they should use a specific strategy—and use it?

Chapter 6
Creativity

The creativity quotient scores of Americans have consistently inched downward since 1990, particularly for students from kindergarten through sixth grade (Bronson & Merryman, 2010). In fact, the decrease for kindergarteners through third graders has been the most significant (Kim, 2011). These alarming findings have many likely culprits, but regardless of the root causes, teachers often find themselves caught between the constraints of externally imposed mandates and the need to value and support the creativity of their students (Beghetto, 2007). Yong Zhao (2009, 2012), an internationally known scholar on the implications of globalization and technology in education, notes that in relation to the importance of creativity in the United States' success, standardization and conformity might be harmful to society. He recommends individualized, holistic approaches to education that promote young people's creativity and entrepreneurship.

Some educators make a distinction between *teaching creatively* and *teaching for creativity*. The former refers to using innovative approaches to make learning more engaging and effective, and the latter is defined as forms of teaching that are intended to develop students' own creativity. In actual practice, however, teaching creatively and teaching for creativity are not dichotomized but integrally related (Jeffrey & Craft, 2004). In fact, students' creative abilities are most likely to develop in environments in which the teachers themselves are creative and teach creatively (Dikici, 2014). Regardless of how it is defined or characterized, creativity in the classroom clearly is a hallmark of American education that we can't afford to neglect.

What Research Says About Creativity

From a review of literature on teacher behaviors that influence the development of creative abilities in students, Giselle Esquivel (1995) posits that teachers play an important role in providing an environment conducive to creative learning. Teachers who show a humanistic philosophical orientation, have developed their own creative competencies, and implement specific creative methods and techniques in their classrooms are more effective in enhancing students' creative abilities than teachers who follow more traditional instructional approaches.

Indeed, creativity is teachable. Well-designed creativity training can enhance students' divergent thinking abilities as well as problem-solving or problem-identification skills. One experimental study finds that association instruction (when the teacher uses numbers, pictures, or music to guide the students to link seemingly unrelated items through contrasting, approximation, and analogy) could increase students' poetic creativity, with the effect size ranging from 0.62 to 1.09 (Cheng, Wang, Liu, & Chen, 2010). Another experimental study finds that blended teaching in science (integrating two or more different learning methods or media tools, such as traditional instruction with technology) could significantly increase student creativity in the following four aspects (Chung, Dzan, Shih, Tsai, & Lou, 2012).

1. Enhancing students' creative character traits, such as imaginativeness, originality, flexibility, and motivation

2. Improving students' abilities in the creative process, such as data collection, integration of new and old knowledge for innovative ideas, and further concretizing and verifying ideas

3. Augmenting students' final product design skills, such as their abilities in completing creative work that is valuable and effective

4. Constructing an environment suited for creativity

In reality, teachers in many cases possess an inaccurate concept of what creativity is, and as a consequence, conflicts arise with the classroom behaviors demonstrated by creative students (Aljughaiman & Mowrer-Reynolds, 2005). One study finds that teachers tend to equate creative thinking with divergent thinking—the ability to generate new ideas—but fail to notice the importance of convergent thinking—the ability to organize and connect ideas (Liu & Lin, 2014). Another study indicates that teachers tend to negatively view personality traits associated with creativity (Westby & Dawson, 1995). They instead prefer traits that seem to run counter to creativity, such as conformity and unquestioning acceptance of authority. The adjectives to describe these teachers' conceptions of creative students include *sincere, responsible, industrious, good-natured, reliable*, and *logical*; unfortunately, these characteristics differ from what is most typical of creative learners.

Research shows that teachers' perceptions of teaching for creativity are influenced by a number of factors, such as self-efficacy, environmental encouragement, societal value, and student potential (Rubenstein, McCoach, & Siegle, 2013). Denise de Souza Fleith (2000) examines teacher and student perceptions about attributes of a classroom environment that either enhance or inhibit the development of creativity. The interview findings indicate that both teachers and students believe a classroom environment that promotes creativity gives students choices, accepts different ideas, boosts students' self-confidence, does not impose ideas on students, and provides students with opportunities to become aware of their creativity. On the other hand, in a creativity-inhibiting classroom, students cannot share ideas, mistakes are not tolerated, teachers are controlling, and teachers use excessive structured drills such as worksheets.

How to Move From Research to Practice

Let's begin by characterizing what we mean by *creative thinking* as practiced in a classroom. To this end, Larry Holt and Marcella Kysilka (2006) provide a helpful comparison of critical thinking (covered in chapter 7) and creative thinking, both of which are important in a dynamic classroom learning environment (table 6.1).

Table 6.1: Keywords for Critical Versus Creative Thinking

Critical Thinking	Creative Thinking
Analytic	Generative
Convergent	Divergent
Vertical	Horizontal (lateral)
Probability	Possibility
Judgmental	Nonjudgmental
Focused	Diffused
Objective	Objective and subjective
Left-brained	Right-brained
Verbal	Verbal and visual
Linear	Associative and circular
Reasoned	Novel

The intent of table 6.1 isn't to define creative or critical thinking as more important than the other. Indeed, in a well-balanced education, teachers emphasize both sides of the chart in instruction and student learning. Moreover, in the ideal classroom, critical thinking and creative thinking are integrative and mutually supportive.

In translating such creativity concepts into practice, Bob Jeffrey (2006) identifies several key characteristics of creative teaching and learning:

- Relevance. Learning that is meaningful to the immediate needs and interests of pupils and to the group as a whole.
- Ownership of knowledge. The pupil learns for herself—not the teacher's, examiner or society's knowledge. Creative learning is internalized and makes a difference to the pupil's self.

- Control of learning processes. The pupil is self-motivated, not governed by extrinsic factors, or purely task-oriented exercises.
- Innovation. Something new is created. A major change has taken place—a new skill mastered, new insight gained, new understanding realised, new, meaningful knowledge acquired. A radical shift is indicated, as opposed to more gradual, cumulative learning, with which it is complementary. (pp. 412–413)

Students' creativity is most likely to be developed in a classroom environment in which the teacher teaches creatively and where there is an active and dynamic ethos. Creative instructional materials and approaches can ignite students' interests and desire for learning. Pedagogy characterized by relevancy allows students to see beyond the content and understand what has real meaning for their life. When students are engaged in the decision-making process, they are more likely to take responsibility for their own learning. And when they assume ownership of their learning, they appreciate the value of learning in itself (versus a means for getting a good score) and, thus, invest in attaining knowledge.

There is a distinction between creativity with a "big C" and creativity with a "little c." The big C refers to the creativity of a legendary genius, such as Mozart or Einstein, and the little c pertains to the everyday life of students. Little c can be the ability to solve problems in a novel way or perceive issues from a fresh point of view (Beghetto & Kaufman, 2013). Although the big C plays a role in classrooms, teachers are particularly positioned to improve the little c. To promote creativity, teachers must first develop a creativity-friendly classroom, where they welcome and reward behavior like asking questions, initiating investigations, and promoting flexible thinking. Secondly, teachers can incorporate explicit teaching of the skills and attitudes necessary for creativity into daily instruction. In addition, teachers can help students learn how individuals are creative within the discipline they study (Starko, 2013). Cropley (2001) provides an excellent guide for fostering creativity in the classroom through the promotion of a three-pronged approach: (1) cognitive aspects, (2) personality, and (3) motivation. A *cognitive aspect* includes varied instructional approaches, such as the following:

- Rich and varied experience in many different settings;
- A fund of general knowledge;
- Specialized knowledge;
- Analyzing and synthesizing skills;
- Skills at seeing connections, overlaps, similarities and logical implications (convergent thinking);
- Skills at making remote associations, linking apparently separate fields (bisociating) and forming new gestalts (divergent thinking);
- Preference for accommodating rather than assimilating;
- Ability to recognize and define problems;
- Ability to plan one's own learning and evaluate progress (executive or metacognitive abilities). (Cropley, 2001, p. 148)

Creativity also requires promotion of particular *personality traits* or dispositions in students, including the following:

- Openness to new ideas and experiences;
- Adventurousness;
- Autonomy;
- Ego strength;
- Positive self-evaluation and high self-esteem;
- Acceptance of all (even contradictory) aspects of one's own self;
- Preference for complexity;
- Tolerance of ambiguity. (Cropley, 2001, p. 148)

Finally, teachers should seek to foster *motivation* for learning in students with the following:

- A concept of creativity and a positive attitude to it;
- Curiosity;
- Willingness to risk being wrong;
- Drive to experiment;
- Task commitment, persistence, and determination;
- Willingness to try different tasks;

- Desire for novelty;
- Freedom from domination by external rewards (intrinsic motivation);
- Readiness to accept a challenge; and
- Readiness for risk taking. (Cropley, 2001, pp. 148–149)

Indeed, the development of creativity is multidimensional and involves cognitive functioning, personal characteristics, and motivation. In order to be creative, students need to know the content well enough to be able to formulate novel learning questions and have an idea what approach to use to fill in the gap in knowledge. They also need to develop the attributes of self-direction, stay open to experience, and be flexible with thinking in order to realize their creative potential.

Summary

Sir Ken Robinson's TED Talk "Do Schools Kill Creativity?" has been watched more than thirty million times (Robinson, 2006). There has been an increasing concern about U.S. education stifling creativity. The critics from the business sector suggest that current forms of education fail to promote the kinds of creativity, risk taking, and ingenuity needed for the future economy. People tend to have the misconceptions that creativity is mastered by a small, select group of individuals; it is associated with art or a few special activities, and when it is used in the classroom, it means setting the students free without any teacher control (Azzam, 2009). In reality, nurturing creativity in the classroom takes disciplined and effortful processes that require knowledge, skills, and control, and creativity should be practiced daily in the classroom. To help teachers incorporate creativity into the classroom, we've assembled the following handouts.

Teachers' perceptions of creativity and classroom practices can either promote or hamper students' development of creativity. The handout "Self-Assessment of Creativity" can help teachers self-examine whether they are establishing a classroom that encourages creative learning experiences.

The creation of a classroom environment that truly embraces creative thinking is often deliberate. Teachers can use the handout "Promoting Creativity Through Creative Processes" (page 64) to see how well they do on the strategies listed to help students think creatively.

One way to promote creativity in the classroom is to make it intentional and explicit. The handout "Incorporating Creativity Into the Lesson" (page 65) compiles a number of strategies for this purpose (Center for Excellence in Learning and Teaching, n.d.; de Bono for Schools, 2015; Starko, 2005). The various tools and techniques included in the handout can improve teachers' focus on creative teaching and learning in the classroom.

Researchers have attempted to measure creativity or creative aptitude. One set of well-known and tested criteria was developed by E. Paul Torrance (Runco, Millar, Acar, & Cramond, 2010). They include fluency (number of ideas generated); flexibility, curiosity, and resistance to closure (ability to generate multiple solutions or different categories of ideas); originality and imagination (ability to generate unusual, unique, and novel ideas); and elaboration (ability to add details and extend ideas). Teachers can use the handout "Measuring Creativity" (page 68) to develop rubrics around these domains according to their content areas and grade levels, so as to communicate expectations for student creativity and measure its attributes.

Self-Assessment of Creativity

Do you agree with the following statements?

☐ Yes ☐ No Creativity can be taught.

☐ Yes ☐ No Creativity can be assessed.

☐ Yes ☐ No Creativity is a fundamental skill to be developed in the classroom.

Among the following areas of student skills and abilities, select five that you emphasize most in your classroom instruction and five that you emphasize the least.

Ability to adapt	Communication skills	Individual and autonomous work
Ability to learn	Critical thinking	Knowledge
Ability to work together	Curiosity	Motivation
Accurate recall of notions or facts	Discipline	Responsibility
Active and participative learning	Empathy	Sense of initiative
Basic skills (writing, reading, and counting)	Independence	Students learning from each other

Top 5	Bottom 5

Source: Adapted from Cachia, R., & Ferrari, A. (2010). Creativity in schools: A survey of teachers in Europe. Seville, Spain: European Commission, Joint Research Centre, Institute for Prospective Technological Studies.

Instructional Methods for Differentiation and Deeper Learning © 2016 Solution Tree Press • solution-tree.com
Visit **go.solution-tree.com/instruction** to download this page.

Promoting Creativity Through Creative Processes

	Poor	Fair	Good
Modeling creativity			
Building student self-efficacy in creativity			
Questioning assumptions			
Imagining other viewpoints			
Cross-fertilizing ideas			
Allowing time for creative thinking			
Instructing and assessing creativity			
Rewarding creative ideas and products			
Encouraging sensible risks			
Tolerating ambiguity			
Allowing mistakes			
Teaching self-responsibility			
Delaying gratification (for long-term learning)			
Encouraging idea generation			
Using profiles of creative people			
Encouraging creative collaboration			

Source: Adapted from Sternberg, R. J., & Williams, W. M. (1996). How to develop student creativity. *Alexandria, VA: Association for Supervision and Curriculum Development.*

Incorporating Creativity Into the Lesson

Following are several techniques you can use to integrate creativity into your classroom.

Scamper

This is an acronym that describes a structured, guided way to assist students with creative thinking and problem solving.

- **S**ubstitute: Using a trial-and-error process to try different things out
- **C**ombine: Synthesizing to create something new
- **A**dapt: Changing what is already known or existing practices
- **M**agnify or **M**inimize: Modifying the size, number, or quality of variables for more outcome possibilities
- **P**ut to other uses: Using things for other purposes than originally intended
- **E**liminate or **E**laborate: Removing or adding more details to a particular quality for more outcome possibilities
- **R**everse or **R**earrange: Focusing on opposite or contrary quality, or changing the order or sequence that would affect the target

Brainstorming

This technique provides a thinking process that strives for a nonjudgmental, supportive atmosphere in which idea production can flourish. The four basic rules of brainstorming are:

1. We rule out criticism.
2. We welcome freewheeling.
3. We desire a quantity of ideas.
4. We seek combination and improvement.

Method 635

This technique is related to brainstorming and often is referred to as *brainwriting*. It involves a group of students generating ideas to solve a specific problem or issue. For instance, six students write down three solutions ideas in five minutes. Each student passes the ideas to the student next to him or her for improvement or to add three new ones. The process continues until every student in the group gets a chance to contribute.

Attribute Listing

In this method, the teacher divides the problem or product into key attributes that the students address separately. By identifying key attributes of the problem or product, the teacher can break the task into manageable components that can then spur new combinations of ideas. To illustrate, consider the following.

Example: What are the key attributes of the story?		
Character? _____	Setting? _____	Conflict? _____

If the students slice and dice what they already know and mix the attributes, they can create surprising and creative ideas.

Adding Random Input

This technique generates new perspectives and ideas. In this strategy, the teacher juxtaposes the problem or subject for creative thought with a randomly selected word. By attempting to make connections between the subject and the unrelated word, students can escape from restrictive thinking patterns and see the problem from a new vantage point or generate new ideas.

Consider the following example. Students are reflecting on their understanding of the responsibilities, duties, privileges, and rights of citizenship. They can select a random noun, whether from a prepared set, from a dictionary, or from words available on the classroom bookshelf. The word can even be from outside the field being studied, such as *ants*. Brainstorming and making associations from there, the class can generate a number of new ideas. For example, the students extrapolate their knowledge about ant colonies to human societies to talk about division of labor, social classes, and privilege that comes with birth.

Six Hats

Six hats (de Bono for Schools, 2015) is a quick, simple technique to help students (or anyone, for that matter) improve and organize their thinking. The six hats refer to the kind of thinking students are engaging in at any given time. As each student is working on a problem, he or she places one of the hats on his or her head to determine what kind of thinking to use. The hats can be either imaginary or phased from de Bono for Schools (2015). The six hats are as follows.

1. The **white hat** calls for information known or needed. This involves data gathering and objective thinking. What are the facts?
2. The **red hat** signifies feelings, hunches, emotions, and intuition. This allows the thinker to use feelings and intuition without justifications.
3. The **black hat** is used for judgment and caution. It is a very valuable hat. The purpose of black hat thinking is to point out why suggestions might not be appropriate for this situation. This is the logic hat.
4. The **yellow hat** symbolizes brightness and optimism. It means positive, logical thinking. The hat allows the user to determine what will work and what it will offer in terms of benefits.
5. The **green hat** focuses on creativity. It entails statements of provocation and investigation.
6. The **blue hat** is used to manage the thinking processes. This is the metacognitive hat. It solves questions like, What is the goal? How are we doing?

Sources: Adapted from Center for Excellence in Learning and Teaching. (n.d.). Techniques for creative teaching. *Accessed at www.celt.iastate.edu/teaching-resources/classroom-practice/teaching-techniques-strategies/creativity/techniques-creative-teaching on October 6, 2014; de Bono for Schools. (2015).* Six thinking hats: A tool to strengthen critical thinking, collaboration, communication, and creativity skills. *Accessed at www.debonoforschools.com/asp/six_hats.asp on July 15, 2015; Starko, A. J. (2005).* Creativity in the classroom: Schools of curious delight *(3rd ed.). Mahwah, NJ: Erlbaum.*

Measuring Creativity

	4	3	2	1
Fluency (Student lists more than five new ideas.)				
Flexibility (Student generates different categories of ideas and has perceptions from different points of view.)				
Originality and Imagination (Student's ideas are interesting and make new contributions that include identifying a previously unknown problem, issue, or solution.)				
Elaboration (Student's ideas are presented with details drawn from a wide variety of resources and important concepts from different contexts and disciplines.)				

Source: Adapted from Runco, M. A., Millar, G., Acar, S., & Cramond, B. (2010). Torrance tests of creative thinking as predictors of personal and public achievement: A fifty-year follow-up. Creativity Research Journal, 22(4), 361–368.

Chapter 7
Critical Thinking

Of the unique skills essential for success in the 21st century, surely one must be the capacity to process and make sense of vast amounts of information on a daily basis. Just coping with an information-rich world requires students to find information, evaluate its trustworthiness, and apply it appropriately within a given context. Developing this effective thinking skill set in a dynamic and rapidly evolving world must be a priority of 21st century schools.

Critical thinking is "reasonable and reflective thinking which uses a variety of skills to reach logical, unbiased and informed reasons or conclusions" (Kysilka & Biraimah, 1993, p. 119). Similarly, Yigal Rosen and Maryam Tager (2014) define critical thinking as:

> The capacity of an individual to effectively engage in a process of making decisions or solving problems by analyzing and evaluating evidence, arguments, claims, beliefs, and alternative points of view; synthesizing and making connections between information and arguments; interpreting information; and making inferences using reasoning appropriate to the situation. (p. 252)

Another detailed definition is given by the aptly named Critical Thinking Community (n.d.):

> The intellectually disciplined process of actively and skillfully conceptualizing, applying, analyzing, synthesizing, and/or evaluating information gathered from, or generated by, observation, experience, reflection, reasoning, or communication, as a guide to belief and action. In its exemplary form, it is based on universal intellectual values that transcend subject matter divisions: clarity, accuracy, precision, consistency, relevance, sound evidence, good reasons, depth, breadth, and fairness.

Regardless of the depth of the definition, thinking critically is a combination of knowledge, skills (or processes), and attitudes. Critical thinkers have many intellectual virtues and habits of mind in common; they are truth seeking, open minded, inquisitive, curious, and analytical, just to name a few (İskifoğlu, 2014). In particular, Donald Orlich, Robert Harder, Richard Callahan, and Harry Gibson (2001) state that effective thinking requires particular attitudes, especially the following:

- Willingness to suspend judgment until sufficient evidence is presented (p. 277)
- Tolerance of ambiguity and uncertainty (p. 277)
- A tendency to question rather than simply accept authority (p. 277)
- Willingness to believe credible evidence (p. 277)
- The capacity to distinguish relevant from irrelevant data, verifiable from nonverifiable data, and problems from irrelevant statements (p. 315)

Furthermore, the Critical Thinking Community (n.d.) states that a student who has been taught to think critically:

- Formulates vital questions and problems clearly and precisely
- Gathers and assesses relevant information
- Generates well-reasoned conclusions and solutions and tests them against relevant criteria and standards

- Thinks open-mindedly within alternative systems of thought
- Is able to recognize and assess assumptions, implications, and practical consequences
- Communicates effectively with others to figure out solutions to complex problems

Effective teachers are often themselves critical thinkers. Critical thinkers understand that one of the major purposes of schooling is to prepare students to meet the challenges of a world shaped by changing forces of technology and globalization (Gouthro & Holloway, 2013).

The more knowledge one has about an object of interest, the more effectively one can think about it. However, given the extraordinarily wide and deep knowledge streams that surround us, information overload can impede effective thinking about almost any issue. What does effective thinking entail in an information-rich age? Perhaps at its most simplistic level, it means an individual must engage actively with data, materials, topics, concepts, and problems in order to think about and make sense of any issue. Developing critical-thinking skills addresses this complex and important matter; thus, it is vital that teachers build effective thinking skills in their students.

What Research Says About Critical Thinking

Lisa Tsui's (1999, 2002) studies reveal that a student's self-assessed growth in critical thinking is *positively* related to teachers' instructional factors, such as assigning writing tasks that demand more analysis and less description, engaging students in classroom discussions, having student papers critiqued by an instructor then requiring rewriting to incorporate feedback, and having students conduct independent research, work on a group project, give a class presentation, and take essay exams. The studies reveal one factor relates *negatively* to increased critical thinking—taking multiple-choice exams, which are easy to use but are not comprehensive and do not require students to provide justifications. An earlier study by Daryl Smith (1977) also associates the teacher's techniques with student gains in critical thinking. For instance, critical thinking consistently and positively relates to the extent to which the teacher encourages, praises, and uses student ideas, the amount and cognitive level of student participation in the classroom, and the level of interaction among students in a course.

Rosen and Tager's (2014) study notes that the Evidence-Centered Concept Map strategy positively correlates with fourteen-year-old students' critical-thinking skills ($r = 0.62$), particularly the skills of assessing and classifying information, recognizing patterns, identifying and prioritizing main ideas, comparing and contrasting, identifying relationships, and thinking logically. (Note: For research in social sciences, a correlation of 0.70 to 1.0 is considered to be very strong, 0.40 to 0.69 as strong, 0.30 to 0.39 as moderate, 0.20 to 0.29 as weak, and 0.01 to 0.19 as negligible.) The Evidence-Centered Concept Map, in particular, helps students gather various claims and evidence from the resources provided, organize the claims with supporting evidence gathered in the previous phase, link claims, and specify the kind of relationship between claims. Other studies also confirm that concept maps can facilitate critical thinking (see Harris & Zha, 2013).

Siu Cheung Kong (2014) finds that purposeful instructional intervention in the classroom (such as having students undertake worksheet questions specifically related to critical-thinking skills) can increase students' skills on hypothesis identification, induction, deduction, explanation, and evaluation. Goal instruction (such as providing an explicit explanation about the specific goal of a discussion) also positively impacts students' reasoning and argumentation in an interactive context (Nussbaum, 2005). Using goal instruction to teach persuasion and reasoning means students become better at arguing their points.

Research on cognitive apprenticeship (Coiro, 2011; Collins, Brown, & Holum, 1991; Powell & Stansell, 2014) posits that teachers can employ the traditional process of apprenticeship to teach students the trade of critical thinking. This process involves four stages to move learners from dependent to independent status.

1. **Modeling:** Modeling allows students to observe by reading or by listening to the teacher's thinking process.

2. **Coaching:** Coaching allows the teacher to observe students in order to provide assistance when necessary.
3. **Scaffolding:** Scaffolding is the support the teacher offers the students to help them successfully complete the task.
4. **Fading:** In a process called fading, teachers eventually remove scaffolding when students no longer need it.

Cognitive apprenticeship is a process, where the teacher, considered the master of critical thinking, teaches complex skills to novices—the students. It involves making the tacit thinking procedures explicit so that students can observe, practice, and reproduce with teacher's feedback and reminders. As they are becoming skilled enough to perform the skills at the master level, the teacher will gradually withdraw help.

How to Move From Research to Practice

Critical thinking is relatively easy to understand once we parse the various factors included in the definitions. However, the more important and complex undertaking is to teach such concepts.

A simple, practical approach is to focus on the mental processes that comprise critical thinking. Orlich et al. (2001) propose just such a set of thinking skills (or thinking processes), which include observing; identifying patterns, relationships, cause-and-effect relationships, assumptions, reasoning errors, logical fallacies, and biases; establishing criteria and classifying; comparing and contrasting; inferring and interpreting; summarizing; analyzing, synthesizing, and generalizing; and hypothesizing and imagining.

Robert Ennis (2000a, 2000b) offers a useful set of suggestions that can help teachers guide students in learning and practicing critical-thinking skills. These eleven suggestions are applicable to students of all age groups and of different achievement levels, and various subject areas. Even young learners are capable of developing critical-thinking skills if the teachers provide support and require effort and perseverance of student thinking (Ennis, 2000b).

1. "Emphasize students' alertness for alternatives" through the learning ("alternative hypotheses, conclusions, explanations, sources of evidence, points of view, plans").
2. Emphasize students "seeking reasons and evidence." Frequently ask questions such as, "Why?" and, "Would you say a little more about that?" in a nonthreatening way whether the teacher agrees, disagrees, or is unsure.
3. Emphasize students "seeing things from others' points of view," being open-minded, and being willing to reconsider other reasons and evidence.
4. Knowledge of subject matter and thinking critically about the subject can proceed together, and sometimes are interdependent. "Students will learn best the subject matter they use. But ultimately, of course, familiarity with the subject and situation calling for critical thinking is essential for critical thinking."
5. Ask students to discuss questions (in the subject area) that are open-ended or even controversial.
6. Give students time to think about a question. If one waits long enough, someone will offer an answer.
7. "Label answers with the student's name" (such as when writing the statement on the board), so that the students can see that teachers acknowledge their thinking, and they will assume some responsibility. "Encourage them to speak up about each other's positions, including giving reasons."
8. Get students to write down their positions, providing reasons to support claims and "showing awareness of opposing positions and the weaknesses of their own positions."
9. Have students read each other's papers, make suggestions, and revise.
10. "Provide a set of criteria for judging students' written position papers" or have students develop the criteria.
11. Model critical thinking.

Fortunately, like many other competencies, teachers can develop critical thinking in their students. Linda Elder and Richard Paul (1996) share a six-stage theory through which teachers can foster the various elements of critical thinking (figure 7.1).

This figure indicates that critical thinking is a process that can be taught and learned. Thinking skills are not innate; on the contrary, it takes deliberate effort to develop these skills. Understanding that students typically go through stages of development in critical thinking can help teachers better predict and identify the barriers in students' intellectual development and therefore better design appropriate instruction to support students. For instance, for reflective thinkers (who are largely unaware of the determining role that thinking is playing in their lives) and for challenged thinkers (who become initially aware of the role of thinking but are unable to identify the flaws in their thinking), teachers can purposefully raise the awareness that quality thinking requires regular practice. The teacher can also explicitly show students that thinking usually involves concepts, assumptions, perspectives, inferences, and implications. In addition, the teacher can explicitly explain the criteria that are usually used to assess thinking, such as clarity, accuracy, coherence, and relevance.

Kong (2014) provides a five-category framework for critical thinking.

1. **Hypothesis identification:** Recognizing the underlying ideas or unstated assumptions of the problem to be addressed
2. **Induction:** Reasoning the connections among a set of specific examples to derive a reliable generalization of the problem
3. **Deduction:** Reasoning the connections among a set of general statements to reach a logically certain conclusion for the problem
4. **Explanation:** Arguing ideas through clarifying the causes, contexts, and consequences of the facts among different aspects of the problem
5. **Evaluation:** Using a set of relevant criteria to determine the quality of the arguments and outcomes related to the problem

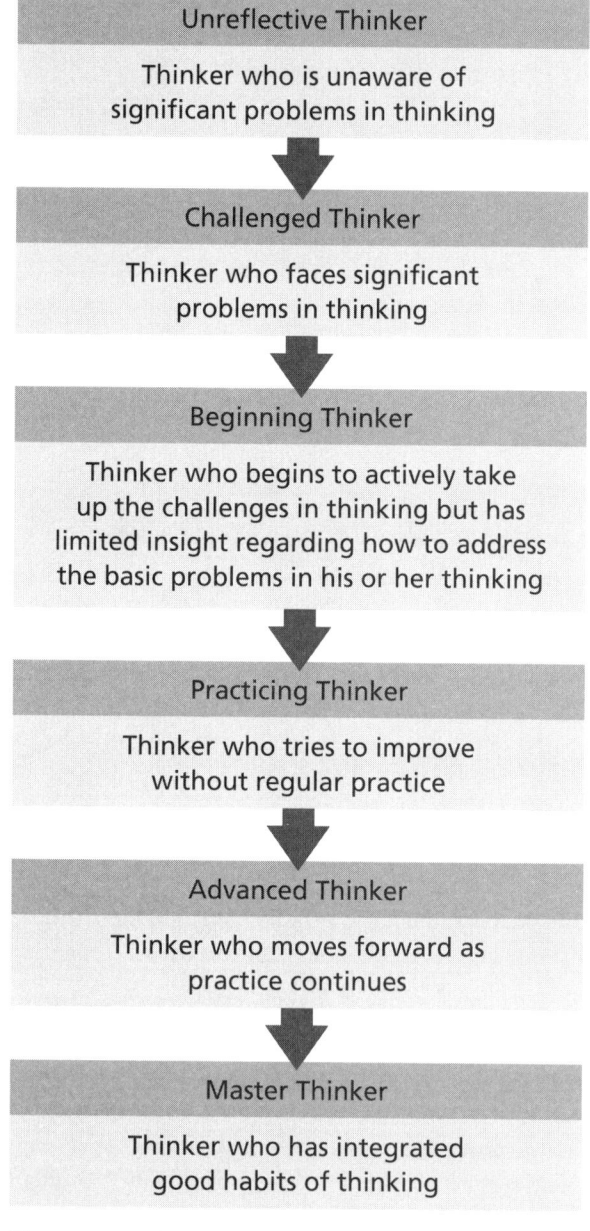

Figure 7.1: Six-stage critical-thinking process.

Again, these five categories indicate critical thinking is the capacity to think reflectively and judge thoughtfully, so as to decide the credibility of the information and what actions to take during reasoning and problem solving. Teachers can tackle one aspect at a time, and it is important to make sure students have sufficient time to think and reflect. Teachers can have students examine poor and sound examples of thinking and talk about the differences. Teachers can also incorporate cooperative learning so that students have more opportunities in small groups to build on each other's thinking and expound on their own thinking.

Diane Halpern (1998) argues that there are clearly identifiable critical-thinking skills that are teachable, and students can learn to recognize and apply them appropriately. She proposes the following taxonomy of critical-thinking skills.

- **Verbal-reasoning skills:** This category includes those skills students need to comprehend, analyze, and evaluate information (in the form of language) to form ideas, beliefs, assumptions, and to develop knowledge. The sources of language can be reading, writing, speaking, and listening.
- **Argument-analysis skills:** An argument is a set of statements with at least one conclusion and one reason that supports the conclusion. This category includes skills for distinguishing claims and counterclaims, supporting reasons with evidence, evaluating others' reasons, and generating counterarguments to others' reasons.
- **Hypothesis-testing skills:** This focuses on the skills to act like scientists to explain, predict, and control events. These skills include recognition of the need for an adequately large sample size, reliability and validity in measurements, and the ability to generalize findings, among others.
- **Skills that determine likelihood and uncertainty:** Because very few events in life can be known with certainty, the correct understanding and use of likelihood and probability is essential in uncertain situations.
- **Decision-making and problem-solving skills:** This category refers to skills in generating decisions and selecting from alternatives based on relevant criteria; problem-solving skills refer to skills in finding solutions to a situation.

The best way to integrate the instruction of thinking with the instruction of subject content, as Matthew Lipman (1991) states, is adding thinking "to the existing course of studies as easily as we add vitamins to our diet" (p. 2). For instance, for the subject of social studies, when teaching the concept of conflict of interests in the human society, the teacher can have students search the Internet for information on positions on a controversial issue by two different stakeholders, and describe and compare their rationale and justification. In this way, students can learn subject content in social studies, practice their literacy skills, and also perform critical thinking.

Even within all of these overarching categories, critical thinking may manifest itself differently depending on subject area and context (Holt & Kysilka, 2006). For instance, mathematics often requires deductive reasoning, whereas inductive strategies are generally preferable in the sciences. In social studies, students are more likely to need skills in cause and effect and verbal reasoning, and in language arts, they may frequently use language or character analysis to determine meaning in a piece of literature. Thus, teachers must know what works best with the content and with their individual students.

Summary

Critical thinking generally encompasses the skills of analyzing arguments, claims, and assumptions; making inferences using inductive or deductive reasoning; judging or evaluating; making decisions or solving problems (Lai, 2011). Critical thinking is recognized as essential for students who need to be prepared for increasing complex life and work environments in the 21st century. As reiterated in this chapter, critical thinking is moldable and malleable by a teacher's intentional instruction. To help teachers train students to think critically, we've included the following handouts.

Critical thinking is a process for mindful learning. Researchers posit that critical thinking and mindfulness are interchangeable. Mindfulness entails the continuous understanding of new information, as well as openness and awareness of more than one perspective (Rosen & Tager, 2014). Teachers play a crucial role in awakening mindfulness and stimulating critical thinking. We adapted and expanded on Halpern's (1998) ideas in the handout "Questions That Make Students Mindful" (page 75) to provide teachers with a number of questions for prompting students to attend to problems or arguments at a deeper level.

Rose Gong (2005) posits that the essence of critical thinking is "the combination of critical thinking skills and the dispositions of fairness, objectivity, impartiality, and nonarbitrariness" (p. 40). The handout "Student Self-Assessment of Disposition and Metacognition in Critical Thinking" (page 78) helps students reflect on their own attitudes toward critical thinking. Do note that we designed this handout for secondary students, so teachers may need to adjust the language for younger students.

The "Checklist of Critical-Thinking Skills" (page 79) draws on Stephen DeLoach and Steven Greenlaw's (2005) synthesis of research and categorizes critical-thinking skills into four levels, moving from more basic thinking to more advanced thinking. (The original model has six levels. The researchers oriented levels 5 and 6 toward postsecondary students and, in general, they are not practical for K–12 settings.) The checklist can serve as operational guidance for teachers to plan for critical-thinking teaching or to assess students' current skills in it. Teachers can also adapt it to self-assess the lesson.

Questions That Make Students Mindful

Could you draw a diagram or other graphic display that organizes the information? (This sort of task makes the structure of a problem or argument clear.)

☐ Does apply   ☐ Does not apply

Notes:

Could you interpret the information presented in your own words? (Paraphrasing can help students construct meaning from instructional messages in their own ways.)

☐ Does apply   ☐ Does not apply

Notes:

Could you summarize the major points of the information? (Writing a short summary is an effective way to prompt students to synthesize information and distinguish between the major themes and the supportive materials.)

☐ Does apply   ☐ Does not apply

Notes:

Detect the inconsistencies in the presented information. Do any of the reasoning procedures contain inaccuracies? (Not all information that students are exposed to is perfect. Being able to critique the consistency and accuracy of information is an important skill to have.)

☐ Does apply   ☐ Does not apply

Notes:

What additional information would you want before answering the question? (This requires the students to think about what is missing from the information they receive.)

☐ Does apply   ☐ Does not apply

Notes:

Explain why you selected a particular alternative. Which alternative is second best? Why? (When students give reasons, it's a good way to focus on the thinking that went into an answer rather than the answer itself.)

☐ Does apply   ☐ Does not apply

Notes:

State the problem in at least two ways. (Most real-world problems are fuzzy; that is, there really are potentially many problems, each with its own possible solution.)

☐ Does apply   ☐ Does not apply

Notes:

Which information is most important? Which information is least important? Why? (The question focuses the students' attention on the value of different sorts of information.)

☐ Does apply   ☐ Does not apply

Notes:

List two solutions for the problem. (This encourages a more creative approach.)

☐ Does apply   ☐ Does not apply

Notes:

What is wrong with an assertion the question makes? (This reminds the students that problems often contain misleading information.)

☐ Does apply   ☐ Does not apply

Notes:

Present two reasons that support the conclusion and two reasons that do not support the conclusion. (Questions of this sort do not permit black-and-white reasoning.)

☐ Does apply   ☐ Does not apply

Notes:

Identify the type of persuasive technique that is used. Is it valid, or is it designed to mislead the reader? Explain your answer. (Students are required to consider the motives and credibility of their information source when responding to these questions.)

☐ Does apply   ☐ Does not apply

Notes:

Compare the two sets of ideas and identify the similarities and differences in terms of the sets' assumptions and inferences. (Comparing can encourage approaching points of view in a more refined way.)

☐ Does apply   ☐ Does not apply

Notes:

What two actions would you take to improve the design of a study described to you? (Students need to think about better types of evidence or procedures that might have provided different results.)

☐ Does apply   ☐ Does not apply

Notes:

Source: Adapted from Halpern, D. F. (1998). Teaching critical thinking for transfer across domains: Dispositions, skills, structure training, and metacognitive monitoring. American Psychologist, 53(4), 449–455.

Student Self-Assessment of Disposition and Metacognition in Critical Thinking

	Which Best Fits Me?		
	Poor	Fair	Well
I am willing to engage in and persist at a complex task.			
I care about what is true and what is false.			
I suppress impulsive reactions and use plans and strategies for my actions.			
I am willing to justify my claims and decisions with evidence.			
I stay open-minded with new information and flexible with my ideas.			
I am aware that alternatives of thinking exist, and I seek them out.			
I am willing to consider other points of view and change my position.			
I provide justifications when I offer a counterargument to others.			
I avoid intimidating and confusing others when I share my argument.			
I reflect on my thinking and am willing to abandon unproductive strategies.			
I like being well informed, and I think it is important to assess the credibility of the information I receive.			
I enjoy reading the collected information on an issue or topic.			
I seek and offer reasons, and I evaluate those reasons.			
I ask and answer questions of clarification, such as *why*, *what*, and *how* questions.			
I withhold judgment until I have sufficient evidence and reasons to support it.			
I am always wondering, seeking problems, and investigating.			
I am sensitive to my own biases.			
I am objective about the inquiry, even if the findings do not support my interest or my preconceived opinions.			

Checklist of Critical-Thinking Skills

Level	Student Skills Checklist
Level 1 **Unilateral Descriptions** (Students paraphrase information, as well as repeat and restate the question.)	☐ Defines terms ☐ Simply repeats information ☐ Uses simple "good" or "bad" statements ☐ Adds little or nothing new to the issue or question
Level 2 **Simplistic Alternatives or Arguments** (Students take a side and do not explore other alternatives; they make unsupported assertions; they make simplistic arguments.)	☐ Includes an assertion, without evidence, often in the form of a question that modestly advances thinking ☐ Challenges an assertion but without evidence ☐ Includes facts (beyond defining terms) relevant to the discussion but no argument ☐ Uses simple explanations, such as giving an example ☐ Cites simple rules or laws as proof ☐ Does not address conflicts with opposing views or does not explore them
Level 3 **Basic Analysis** (Students make a serious attempt to analyze an argument or competing arguments, and evaluate it or them with evidence.)	☐ Appeals to a recognized (appropriate) authority ☐ Includes casual observation, anecdotal recollections, or data ☐ Includes assertions with explicit evidence offered or a reasoned challenge of another's assertion, but without a clear logical framework ☐ Uses a singular, Socratic-style question ☐ Often lists numerous factors as evidence, but does not integrate them within a logical framework ☐ Does not have a clear conclusion or choice between alternatives; for instance, when pressed for the best explanation, student responds that both (or all) are equally valid
Level 4 **Inference** (Students make a cohesive argument.)	☐ Includes logical statements based on the discipline's accepted mode or schools of thought ☐ Identifies assumptions ☐ Challenges a key assumption of another's theory ☐ Includes a series of logical, Socratic-style questions ☐ Searches for data to test the validity of an argument ☐ Integrates data with consistency to support an argument in oral or written language

Source: Adapted from DeLoach, S. B., & Greenlaw, S. A. (2005). Do electronic discussions create critical thinking spillovers? Contemporary Economic Policy, 23(1), 149–163.

Chapter 8
Complex Thinking

What do students really need to learn in order to succeed, not only in the classroom but also later on in college, the workplace, and as engaged citizens? Beginning in 2010, a movement for deeper learning or complex thinking has emerged on the United States' education scene. *Complex thinking* refers to a set of competencies students must master in order to develop keen understanding of academic content and apply their knowledge to novel tasks and situations in the classroom and on the job—competencies such as problem finding, problem solving, and creative thinking (Huberman, Bitter, Anthony, & O'Day, 2014). Students need to develop attitudes and mindsets that empower them to confront new challenges, take the initiative, and persevere through setbacks.

Unfortunately, the academic rigor of teaching and learning in many classrooms is low. Teachers do not always have enough time or the expertise to balance the memorization of facts with the more complex tasks of applying, synthesizing, evaluating, and communicating. A review of the Third International Mathematics and Science Study (TIMSS) 1999 video study finds that mathematics teachers in the United States focus learning on content, routine exercises, and procedures at the lower end of the cognitive continuum (Hiebert et al., 2005). Additionally, U.S. students spend 34 percent of each mathematics lesson applying knowledge as compared to 74 percent for Japanese students.

Surface learning of factual knowledge is necessary in any subject or content area, but the learning should not stop at that level. Effective teachers understand how to deepen student learning from the simple to the complex and emphasize how to find meaning and be mindful. They present content at different levels of complexity, employing a wide repertoire of objectives and strategies, and developing activities and questions that target higher and lower cognitive levels so that students can master both content and the level of thinking required for the content. They scaffold lessons, provide feedback, and suggest learning strategies to guide students to begin skill and knowledge acquisition. They use step-by-step instructions, modeling, and opportunities for students to apply new information and skills to novel situations (Zahorik, Halbach, Ehrle, & Molnar, 2003). Finally, they recognize the complexities of the subject matter and focus on meaningful conceptualization of knowledge rather than on isolated facts (Mason, Schroeter, Combs, & Washington, 1992; Wenglinsky, 2004). Thus, in this chapter, we will explore how to improve cognitive complexity of lessons to encourage deeper learning.

What Research Says About Complex Thinking

One study on elementary and middle school students' academic performance finds that those who receive instruction emphasizing both critical thinking *and* memorization perform better than those whose instruction emphasizes critical thinking *or* memorization (Sternberg, 2003). Students report greater interest, concentration, and enjoyment doing tasks when they perceive a high congruence between the challenges of the task and their own skills (Shernoff, Csikszentmihalyi, Schneider, & Shernoff, 2003). According to flow theory, flow is "a state of deep absorption in an activity that is intrinsically enjoyable, as when artists or athletes are focused on their play or performance," and individuals in this state function at their fullest capacity and perceive "their performance to be pleasurable and successful, and the activity is perceived as worth doing for its own sake, even if no further goal is reached" (Shernoff et al., 2003, p. 160). The state of flow can be achieved among the students when challenges match with the skills needed to meet those challenges.

When teachers match task complexities with students' individual skills, their engagement and motivation rise. However, when teachers do not align tasks to students' skill levels, then engagement and motivation decrease (Csikszentmihalyi et al., 1993). Complex thinking in classrooms directly relates to student cognitive engagement which, in turn, affects students' psychological investment in learning self-regulation strategies. Students who are appropriately challenged tend to have more positive perceptions of competency, be more willing to engage in learning activities and make an effort to learn, establish task-oriented goals, and use more self-regulation strategies like memorization, task planning, and self-monitoring (Archambault, Janosz, Fallu, & Pagani, 2009).

Higher-level instruction can prompt students to make meaningful attempts to process new information and integrate it with existing knowledge in order to form a richer, more coherent mental representation. In contrast, lower-level learning, such as underlining and rote processing of new information, produces a less elaborative memory representation, making it harder for students to later retrieve and transfer the information (Greene, Miller, Crowson, Duke, & Akey, 2004). Teachers who emphasize higher-order thinking can improve the gains in students' reading fluency by an effect size of 0.66 and comprehension by 0.59 (Taylor, Pearson, Peterson, & Rodriguez, 2003). Barbara Taylor et al. (2003) also find that asking higher-level questions contributes to improved student reading achievement, while routine practice on skills, passive responding, and telling are detrimental to advances in reading achievement.

Mette Huberman et al. (2014) find the advantage for students attending a deeper-learning school is equivalent to moving from the 50th to the 54th or 55th percentile in reading, mathematics, and science, as measured by the Programme for International Student Assessment–Based Test for Schools. The survey results from Huberman et al. (2014) suggest that these students are more academically motivated and engaged than the comparison group of students, who do not attend a deeper-learning school. Research also reveals that high versus low cognitive challenge impacts student affect (see table 8.1).

Additional research on complex thinking yields the following results.

- Effective teachers are concerned with having students learn and demonstrate their understanding rather than merely memorizing facts or events (Blackburn, 2013).
- A deep learning approach relates to students' enjoyment of learning and the attitude of finding it important (Göçmençelebi, Özkan, & Bayram, 2012).
- By scaffolding learning activities in a way that moves students from well-structured problems to ill-structured applied problems that encourage more elaborate processing of content, teachers promote deep learning and help students learn to transfer their learning to other contexts (Green, Bean, & Peterson, 2013).

Table 8.1: Students Who Seek Challenges Versus Those Who Avoid Challenges

Students Who Seek High-Level Cognitive Challenges	Students Who Avoid High-Level Cognitive Challenges
Have a higher tolerance for failure	Have a high negative affect after failure
Have a learning goal orientation	Have a performance-focused goal orientation
Have high self-efficacy	Have lower self-efficacy
Use deep learning strategies (for example, use critical-thinking skills to look for meaning in the content and relate it to personal experiences and ideas)	Have a greater use of shallow or surface strategies (for example, strategies requiring minimal processing of information)

Source: Adapted from Meyer, Turner, & Spencer, 1997.

- When teachers develop learning materials based on the theory of reasoning and understanding, students experience in-depth learning and improved knowledge gains, structure, and retention. High-level cognitive activities can facilitate deep understanding of complex and abstract concepts (Reinfried, Aeschbacher, & Rottermann, 2012).

The research generally finds that students are able to take on challenging and complex thinking if teachers' instruction is designed to elicit the use of higher-level thinking strategies.

How to Move From Research to Practice

Based on extensive interviews with experts in the field of education and a review of the relevant literature, a study supported by the William and Flora Hewlett Foundation (2013) identifies six dimensions of complex thinking that must become a part of classroom instruction.

1. **Mastery of core academic content:**
    - Students understand key principles and relationships within a content area and organize knowledge in a concept framework.
    - They are able to remember and recall facts relevant to a content area but also possess procedural knowledge and understand how content knowledge is produced and how experts solve problems.
    - They can apply facts, processes, and theories to real-world situations.
2. **Critical thinking and problem solving:**
    - Students are familiar with and able to use tools and techniques gleaned from core subjects to formulate and solve problems, which include data analysis, reasoning, scientific inquiry, nonlinear thinking, and persistence.
3. **Effective communication:**
    - Students cooperate to complete tasks and solve problems.
    - They work in groups to identify collective goals and incorporate different points of view to meet them.
4. **Collaboration:**
    - Students organize their data, findings, and thoughts in meaningful and useful ways.
    - They communicate ideas in both written and oral presentations. They are able to provide constructive feedback to peers as well as incorporate feedback from others.
5. **Learning how to learn:**
    - Students set goals for learning, monitor their progress toward them, and adapt their learning approach as needed.
    - They know and can apply a variety of study skills and strategies to meet the demands of a task.
    - They anticipate and are prepared to meet changing expectations in a variety of academic and social environments.
6. **Academic mindsets:**
    - Students develop positive attitudes and beliefs about themselves as learners.
    - They have academic perseverance and engage in productive academic behaviors.
    - They perceive the inherent value of content learning and see the relevance of schoolwork to their lives and future well-being.

An example focusing on the second dimension of the preceding framework, *critical thinking and problem solving*, helps illustrate what complex thinking looks like in real life. At Anson High School in Wadesboro, North Carolina—a school of the New Tech Network, which is dedicated to ensuring students develop the skills necessary to thrive in college, careers, and civic life—teachers operate as facilitators rather than dispensers of information (Vander Ark & Schneider, 2014). They work in multidisciplinary teams; for instance, the teachers of world geography and earth science work together, as do those of American literature and U.S. history, and world literature and world history. They establish blocks of time so that students can take on big questions that force them to sort and synthesize multiple sources of information and to select the most appropriate problem-solving and presentation tools. For example, the students in one small, extremely poor, rural community participate in a schoolwide farm project (GettingSmart, 2014). They create their own agribusiness and present plans to a team for review before implementation. They use hydroponics, aquaponics, and other techniques of sustainable farming. They also use solar power and other alternative energy sources for the greenhouse and other energy needs. These learning opportunities integrate real-world problems with curriculum, allowing students to think deeply, work collaboratively, and communicate effectively while mastering academic content at the same time.

Based on a review of reports on workplace skill demands, the National Research Council (2012) identifies three broad domains of competence for 21st century skills. First is *cognitive*, which includes cognitive processes and strategies, knowledge, and creativity. Next is *intrapersonal*, which involves intellectual openness, work ethic and conscientiousness, and positive self-evaluation. Last is *interpersonal*, which includes teamwork, collaboration, and leadership. These three domains actually are aligned well with the six dimensions presented previously.

1. **Cognitive:** Mastery of core academic content + Critical thinking and problem solving

2. **Intrapersonal:** Learning how to learn + Academic mindset

3. **Interpersonal:** Effective communication + Collaboration

Although we delineate three or six distinctive domains or dimensions, complex thinking usually is a product or mechanism that involves all these intertwined elements to function together. Cognitive learning can be enhanced by the intrapersonal skills used to reflect on one's learning and adjust learning strategies (similar to the metacognition we discussed in chapter 5). In addition, the interpersonal skills of communicating verbal and nonverbal messages and staying open-minded about other persons' viewpoints can also support cognitive learning.

As teachers plan to incorporate complex thinking in their classrooms, they should integrate knowledge, skills, and attitudes in their instruction so that students can grow holistically (Baartman & de Bruijn, 2011). It's also important to increase the rigor of teaching. Rigor creates an environment in which teachers expect each student to learn at high levels, support each student so he or she can learn at high levels, and acknowledge each student's demonstration of learning at high levels (Blackburn, 2013). In other words, rigor is about integrating expectations, instructional effectiveness, and assessment practices (Blackburn, 2013).

Teachers should also use scaffolded instruction, which is a constructive approach to learning that allows students to accept mistakes. Scaffolded instruction and the proximity of teacher support can create a sense of intellectual safety in the classroom that encourages students to take the academic risks necessary for meaningful learning to occur.

Moderate levels of challenge are essential for maximizing learning and optimizing motivation. *Challenge* implies there are considerable chances for student errors. Thus, teachers should avoid creating an error-proof learning environment and instead strive to maintain appropriate task difficulty, attend to errors, recognize failed attempts, address faulty performances, and sustain the quality of assessment. According to Margaret Clifford (1990), teachers must respect imperfect student work in order to "replace easy success with challenge" and grant students the privilege to "reach beyond their intellectual grasp" and learn from mistakes, rather than using easy success as the yardstick to measure learning (p. 23).

Above all, teachers should teach for meaning. This means helping students perceive the relationship of parts (the discrete skills) to the whole (the application of skills to communicate, comprehend, or reason). It's important to provide students with the tools to construct meaning in their encounters with academic tasks in school, and also in the world in which they live. This way, they can more easily make real-world connections (Knapp, Shields, & Turnbull, 1995).

Summary

The competencies in conducting complex cognitive thinking are consistently and positively related to an individual's education and career outcomes. The 21st century needs more than disparate, superficial facts or procedures; it requires well-integrated knowledge and skills that are transferable to solve new problems (Pellegrino & Hilton, 2012). To help teachers incorporate complex thinking into their classrooms, we've compiled the following set of handouts.

The checklist "Deepen the Instruction" (page 86) builds on the work of Thomas Good and Jere Brophy (2007) and provides a number of prompts for teachers to assess the depth of their instruction. It includes items not just for factual learning but also for more challenging and complex forms of learning. Teachers can use the checklist to reflect—either when planning a new unit or after finishing teaching a unit.

Research in education sometimes seems to pit one strategy against another. However, in real life, improving instruction is not as simple as choosing one technique over another. A study by Kenneth Koedinger, Julie Booth, and David Klahr (2013) finds that there are actually more than 205 trillion instructional options available when considering the combinations of different factors. The optimal forms of learning—including complex thinking—depend on the dynamic interaction of content, instruction, and the learners themselves. The handout "Strategy Reflection Activity" (page 88) provides a reflective activity so teachers can internalize selected aspects of the vast amount of instructional information and research.

"The ABC List" (page 89) helps teachers expand their thinking about instructional strategies. This handout asks teachers to name at least one instructional strategy beginning with each letter. Each teacher can think about which strategies are most effective for his or her subject area and grade level. Despite the fact there are more than 205 trillion instructional options, Koedinger et al. (2013) also propose that researchers and teachers should ask themselves questions that focus on how different forms of instruction meet different functional needs, such as:

- Which methods are best for learning memory facts?
- Which methods are best for acquiring skills?
- Which methods are best for learning to make sense of concepts and principles?

Teachers can use the handout "Teacher Self-Assessment" (page 90) to help evaluate their own level of complex thinking in a lesson or unit.

Deepen the Instruction

	None	A Little	Quite a Bit	Completely
Learning Goals				
I express goals in terms of long-term student outcomes (acquisition of knowledge, skills, values, or dispositions they can apply to life outside of school), not just in terms of short-term content mastery.				
Content				
I teach content in sufficient depth to allow students to develop understanding and application.				
I represent knowledge content as a network of related information structured around powerful key ideas.				
In presenting and leading discussions of the content, I help students recognize the centrality of key ideas and use them as the basis around which to structure larger content networks.				
In addition to providing explicit explanations, I ask questions and engage students in activities that require them to process the information actively, test their understanding, and if necessary, repair their understanding and communicate about these repairs.				
Skills				
I teach and use skills (procedural knowledge) in the process of applying information content (propositional knowledge) rather than teaching them as separate entities.				
I embed most skill practices within inquiry, problem solving, decision making, or other whole-task application contexts rather than limiting them to isolated practice.				
When I teach skills, I emphasize modeling their strategic use for accomplishing particular purposes, as well as explain when and why students would use the skills.				

Instructional Methods for Differentiation and Deeper Learning © 2016 Solution Tree Press • solution-tree.com
Visit **go.solution-tree.com/instruction** to download this page.

	None	A Little	Quite a Bit	Completely
Classroom Discourse				
In discourse with my students, I emphasize sustained and thoughtful interactions featuring critical or creative thinking about key ideas, not just fast-moving recitation of specific facts or details.				
Activity and Assessment				
My activities and assignments call for students to integrate or apply key ideas and engage in critical and creative thinking, problem solving, inquiry, decision making, or other higher-order applications, not just to demonstrate recall of facts and definitions.				
I focus my assessment of student learning on understanding and application goals, not just low-level factual memory or skills mastery goals.				

Source: Adapted from Good, T. L., & Brophy, J. E. (2007). Looking in classrooms *(10th ed.). Boston: Allyn & Bacon.*

Strategy Reflection Activity

Term	Student Engagement	Rigor	Complex Thinking	Instructional Strategies
What is the term, and what is your definition of the term?				
What might this look like in your classroom?	Examples of what students do to indicate that they are engaged:	Examples of how you provide rigor in your classroom or school:	Examples of what students do or say that provides evidence of deep learning:	Examples of instructional strategies that you use:
Why is this important?				

The ABC List

A	N
B	O
C	P
D	Q
E	R
F	S
G	T
H	U
I	V
J	W
K	X
L	Y
M	Z

Hint:

Marzano's High-Yield Strategies
(Marzano, Pickering, & Pollock, 2001)

1. Cooperative learning
2. Generating and testing hypotheses
3. Homework and practice
4. Identifying similarities and differences
5. Nonlinguistic representations
6. Questions, cues, and advance organizers
7. Reinforcing effort and providing recognition
8. Setting objectives and providing feedback
9. Summarizing and note taking

Hattie's High-Yield Strategies
(Hattie, 2009)

1. Challenging goals
2. Direct instruction
3. Feedback
4. Questioning
5. Mastery learning
6. Metacognitive strategies, self-verbalization, or self-questioning
7. Reciprocal teaching
8. Teacher expectations
9. Advance organizers

Sources: Hattie, J. (2009). Visible learning: A synthesis of over 800 meta-analyses relating to achievement. New York: Routledge; Marzano, R. J., Pickering, D. J., & Pollock, J. E. (2001). Classroom instruction that works: Research-based strategies for increasing student achievement. Alexandria, VA: Association for Supervision and Curriculum Development.

Teacher Self-Assessment

Which of the following forms of instruction do you use?

Structured learning: Teacher provides the materials, questions, and procedures.

Yes _____ No _____

Guided learning: Teacher provides materials and questions for students to explore, but allows them to develop the procedure.

Yes _____ No _____

Open learning: Teacher allows students to formulate the question to investigate, find the materials, and design the procedure.

Yes _____ No _____

Which of the following learning objectives did you aim to accomplish and to what degree did you succeed (Anderson & Krathwohl, 2001; Guo et al., 2007)?

Knowledge: Teacher stimulates students to recall, describe, recognize, or define the knowledge or information that they have learned and remembered but not necessarily understood.

Yes _____ No _____ Accomplished _____ Not Accomplished _____

Comprehension: Teacher prompts students to understand, explain, summarize, or elaborate on facts, ideas, and principles, and discover the relationship among two or more learning events, such as the ability to understand basic definitions, to make comparisons, and to draw conclusions about general principles.

Yes _____ No _____ Accomplished _____ Not Accomplished _____

Application: Teacher encourages students to apply recently learned knowledge to resolve new problems.

Yes _____ No _____ Accomplished _____ Not Accomplished _____

Analysis: Teacher prompts students to break what they've learned into component parts and infer the relationships among them.

Yes _____ No _____ Accomplished _____ Not Accomplished _____

Synthesis: Teacher encourages students to integrate what they've learned into a single creative response in either an oral or substantive form.

Yes _____ No _____ Accomplished _____ Not Accomplished _____

Evaluation: Teacher encourages students to make value decisions through certain criteria.

Yes _____ No _____ Accomplished _____ Not Accomplished _____

Which of the following instructional strategies did you use, and how well did they help students achieve the learning objectives?

Classifying	Observing
Assuming	Graphing
Comparing	Evaluating
Contrasting	Analyzing
Explaining	Summarizing
Predicting (or hypothesizing)	Authentic questions or materials
Inferring, interpreting data, or drawing conclusions	Communicating
Measuring	Collecting data
Designing an investigation to solve a problem	Experimenting

Comments:

Source: Adapted from Anderson, L. W., & Krathwohl, D. R. (Eds.). (2001). A taxonomy for learning, teaching, and assessing: A revision of Bloom's taxonomy of educational objectives (Complete ed.). New York: Longman; Guo, S.-J., Tsai, C.-H., Chang, F. M.-T., & Huang, H.-I. (2007). The study of questioning skills on teaching improvement. International Journal of Learning, 14(8), 141–145.

Chapter 9
Active Learning

Many of the methods in this book, such as problem-based learning and complex thinking, overlap with active learning to a certain degree. However, active learning is a broader concept and, in practice, does not necessarily follow the processes of the other instructional models.

So what do we mean by *active learning*? Simply put, active learning is the opposite of passive learning. Researchers generally define it as any instructional method that engages students in the learning process. Actively learning students engage in meaningful learning activities and think about what they are doing (Prince, 2004). Passive students, on the other hand, depend on a teacher to impart knowledge, and passive learning requires little student personal involvement or overt work—it is not considered self-reinforcing. Passive learning also tends to get dull very quickly as learners become disinterested, unmotivated, nonresponsive, and ineffectual. Students typically do not well retain information they learn passively, or apply it effectively (Petress, 2008).

Active learners commonly use their teachers as resources, as guides to the learning process, and as motivators for further endeavors. They see learning as enjoyable, motivational, and effective. Additionally, active learning stimulates pride, increases self-efficacy, imparts credibility in the eyes of teachers, helps students stay alert and aware, fuels a thirst for broader and deeper understanding in future academic endeavors, and tends to make learning more fun and personally satisfying (Harmin, 2006; Petress, 2008).

To better understand active learning, it is helpful to identify key attributes of instruction that promote such learning. R. Scott Grabinger and Joanna Dunlap (1995) developed one such set of attributes that nicely describe teaching conducive to active learning (table 9.1).

Table 9.1: Teaching Attributes That Promote Active Learning

Teaching Attributes	Outcomes
Authenticity	Promotes study and investigation within authentic contexts
Sense of agency	Encourages the growth of student responsibility, initiative, decision making, and intentional learning
Collaboration	Cultivates collaborative learning among students and teachers
High-order thinking	Uses dynamic, interdisciplinary, generative learning activities that promote higher-order thinking processes to help students develop rich and complex knowledge structures
Monitoring	Assesses student progress in content and learning to learn within authentic contexts using realistic tasks and performances

By including active learning as a tool in this book, we don't advocate its use in lieu of other instructional approaches. Active learning does not mean that teachers forego direct instruction or that they no longer lead overall learning goals and experiences. In fact, quite the opposite is true: the best teachers plan and implement learning experiences that are well thought out and significantly orchestrated. What we offer is simply evidence that when students engage actively in their own learning, they are more effective learners. In fact, teacher-directed instruction and active learning need not be mutually exclusive. Thus, regardless of the instructional approach that teachers implement in the classroom, students can—and should—be active learners.

What Research Says About Active Learning

Considerable research agrees that active learning has a positive impact on academic attainment and attitudes across a range of subject areas and grade levels (Baepler, Walker, & Driessen, 2014; Köksal, Yagisan, & Aksoy, 2013; Odabaşi & Kolburan, 2013). Onur Köksal and colleagues (2013) find that active learning classrooms promote engagement, enrich students' learning experiences, allow flexibility in approaches to learning, engender confidence in academic tasks, and facilitate learning outcomes. Battal Odabaşi and Güliz Kolburan (2013) note that active learning promotes students' participation, socialization, and cooperation tendencies. Köksal et al. (2013) also find that active learning leads to better learning results and more positive student attitudes than purely teacher-centered learning. Table 9.2 describes the attributes of learner and teacher in active learning.

Furthermore, Köksal et al. (2013) draw a distinction between traditional teacher-centered instruction and active learning, as shown in table 9.3.

Research suggests that appropriate integration of technology, such as the use of tablets and laptops, can improve active learning (Gerard, Knott, & Lederman, 2012). Technology allows teachers and students to handwrite notes, annotate electronic documents, draw pictures, add diagrams, and move items around directly on screen throughout the active learning process. The portability of technology devices allows teachers and students to move beyond the podium and seats without compromising the capability of adding content to the screen. Tablets and laptops provide students with immediate access to outside resources. They also enrich real-time classroom interaction where students' in-class thinking and creation of knowledge can be preserved, and students are more likely to be active participants when their ideas and input are written and recorded.

Table 9.2: Attributes of Learners and Teachers in Active Learning

Learner in Active Learning	Teacher in Active Learning
Self-confident	Guide
Energetic	Observer
Self-regulating	Democratic
Belonging to the group	Supplier
Sensitive	Satisfies curiosity
Determined	Innovative
	Productive

However, research also reveals that it is difficult for teachers to give qualitatively good feedback during active learning (van den Bergh, Ros, & Beijaard, 2013). The researchers observed thirty-two teachers who practiced active learning in the domain of environmental studies in the sixth, seventh, and eighth grades. They found about half of the teacher-student interactions contained feedback. Teachers usually focused this feedback on the tasks that students performed and on the ways in which they processed them. Only 5 percent of the feedback explicitly addressed a learning goal. In the feedback, the teachers directed, rather than facilitated, the learning processes. Although feedback focusing on students' metacognition is effective in improving student learning, and metacognition is both an objective and a means of active learning, teachers gave feedback on students' metacognition in just 1 percent of all teacher-student interactions. So, while active learning is important, teachers must learn how to incorporate it in such a way that includes feedback. The core tenets of effective feedback include timeliness, alignment with the criteria of the task, and actionability (in terms of enabling students to adjust their thinking or strategies).

How to Move From Research to Practice

Research has shown that a high degree of interactivity encourages deeper approaches to learning, and there are a number of techniques that teachers can incorporate into their daily instruction to make it more applied, interactive, and participative (Angelo & Cross, 1993; Morrison-Shetlar & Marwitz, 2001; Silberman, 1996; VanGundy, 2005; Watkins, 2005; Yee, n.d.). Of the many types of interactive strategies

Table 9.3: Comparison of Teacher-Centered Instruction and Active Learning

	Teacher-Centered Instruction	Active Learning
Knowledge	Moves one way—from the teacher to learner	Is constructed by teacher and learner
Learner	Is an empty container to be filled	Is active, constructive, exploratory, and transforming
Teacher	Is an expert	Is a guide and facilitator
Communication	Is initiated and dominated by the teacher	Is reciprocal between teacher and learner
Studying strategy	Is individual, passive, and isolated	Is participative and cooperative

available, we will focus on lectures, individual work, pair and group work, and multimedia.

Lectures

A practical issue for teachers and education leaders to consider is how to enact active learning in a classroom. Given the prominent role that lectures (or minilectures) play in instructional delivery, it is useful to ponder how a lecture can be engaging and yield active learning opportunities for students. To do so, teachers must design the lecture and its related activities around important learning goals and promote thoughtful engagement on the part of the students.

Andrea Revell and Emma Wainwright (2009) titled their study on teaching excellence "What Makes Lectures 'Unmissable'?" Based on interviews with university lecturers and focus groups with undergraduate students, the research team draws the logical conclusion that there is probably no such thing as an entirely unmissable lecture. Nonetheless, they find that three key factors significantly enhance class attendance rates (certainly a criterion for active learning).

1. Provide a high degree of participation and interactivity (active learning) for students in the presentation.
2. Develop and follow a clear structure in the presentation, which enables students to more easily form integrative links (connecting prior learning to the current instruction).
3. Utilize a passionate, enthusiastic instructor who can bring a subject to life for students.

Additional techniques that can help teachers make lectures into more active and engaging learning experiences include the following (Yee, n.d.).

- **Instructor storyteller:** The teacher illustrates a concept, idea, or principle with a real-life application, model, or case study.
- **Empty outlines:** The teacher distributes a partially completed outline of the lesson and asks students to fill it in.
- **Total physical response:** Students either stand or sit to indicate their binary answers, such as *true* or *false*, to the teacher's questions.
- **Response cards:** The teacher distributes standardized cards that students can hold aloft as visual responses to questions.
- **Classroom opinion poll:** The teacher uses informal hand raising to solicit students' opinions. This also allows him or her to examine how polarized the class is before discussing a controversial subject.
- **Everyday ethical dilemmas:** The teacher presents an abbreviated case study with an ethical dilemma related to the subject content.
- **Pop culture:** The teacher infuses the lesson with current events from the pop culture world.
- **Make students guess:** The teacher introduces new content by asking intriguing questions.

Individual Work

There are many ways to infuse active learning into individual student work. For instance, a teacher could introduce one-minute papers, in which students write for one minute on a specific question, such as, "What was the most important thing you learned today?"

Students could also create art to demonstrate understanding; the teacher could have them illustrate an abstract concept.

Following are several more ideas for integrating active learning into individual work (Yee, n.d.).

- **Pro-and-con grid:** Students list the pros and cons for a given subject, topic, or specific lesson.
- **Circle the questions:** The teacher prepares a handout that has a few questions students are likely to have about the content and asks students to circle the ones they do not know the answers to; students tear the questions off and post them on the wall in the order of the question numbers, and the teacher can then see the gaps in student knowledge and respond by prioritizing instruction.
- **Real-world issues:** Students discuss in class how a topic or concept relates to a real-world issue or application. A good way to accomplish this is to pose questions related to contemporary news events (such as elections or sports).
- **Tabloid titles:** Students write a tabloid-style headline that illustrates the content they are learning. Then they share and vote on the best headlines.
- **Bumper stickers:** Students create a slogan-like bumper sticker to illustrate a concept they are learning.

Pair and Group Work

Teachers can also incorporate active learning into pair and group work. The most prevalent is probably think-pair-share, wherein students share and compare possible answers to a question with a partner before addressing the larger class. Forced debate is another way to bring active learning front and center. In this strategy, students debate in pairs, but must defend the opposite side of their personal opinion. Other examples for highlighting active learning in pair and group work include the following (Yee, n.d.).

- **Optimist or pessimist:** Students take opposite emotional sides of a topic while conducting a conversation.
- **Invented dialogues:** Students weave together real quotes from primary sources, or invent ones to fit the speaker and context to demonstrate their knowledge of a point of view or issue, for instance, creating a dialogue between Socrates and Aristotle.
- **Presentation reaction:** The teacher divides the students into four groups after presenting the new content: (1) questioners, (2) example givers, (3) divergent thinkers who disagree with the points of the lecture, and (4) agreers. Students play the roles they are assigned and take different positions accordingly to extend the discussions.

Multimedia

Using multimedia in the classroom is a great way to make learning active. Do note that before engaging students with social media outlets as part of classroom learning experiences, teachers should check and follow school district requirements and guidelines.

Twitter is an ideal social media tool to use in the classroom. With it, students can follow experts in the subject area and stay current with their thinking. They can also write their own tweets that summarize important concepts they have learned, and other students can follow and provide comments.

YouTube is another great tool; it allows access to a wide variety of videos and provides an audience for classroom videos as well. For instance, teachers can use popular clips online to illustrate a point or start a conversation. In order to share active learning ideas, they can also use a camera to record a demonstration relevant to learning and post it on YouTube, or even post videos of students' projects, presentations, or speeches, all while being careful to strictly follow guidelines on posting images of students online.

Teachers can also use wikis to develop great conversations and manage activities, resources, and projects. Wikis, which are free through platforms like www.wikispaces.com, allow students to collaborate in real time. Wikis allow teachers to create projects, assign teams, monitor students' real-time progress, and provide ongoing feedback. At the end of the projects, the students can share the products with the whole class and even with parents. Wikis also provide a safe network for connection and communication. Students can collaboratively edit pages and embed resource links from the web, such as videos, documents, images, and polls. Teachers use wikis to make announcements. They also have the capacity to monitor the complete history of student discussions, writing, and file uploads.

Finally, blogs are a great way to encourage students to write and publish for a wider, real-world audience. Teachers can have students write posts about what they have learned and also comment on each other's entries.

Summary

Learning loses all its enchantment when it is not active. Students learn superficially when they are not actively engaged, and on the other hand, active learning helps students process and retain information. Active learning requires efforts on the part of teachers to plan and execute instruction that keeps students interested and on task and makes learning meaningful and intriguing. To help teachers incorporate active learning into the classroom, several helpful handouts follow.

The handout "Self-Assessment of Active Learning" (page 98) lists behaviors that active learners are likely to demonstrate, based on the five attributes of active learning described by Grabinger and Dunlap (1995). With appropriate modifications for readability and practicality, younger students can also use the tool to assess the extent to which they are engaging in these behaviors. Additionally, teachers can use the tool to assess for the five attributes in their teaching.

As discussed earlier, the core of active learning is incorporating activities that help students develop deep understanding of the important ideas they must learn. One popular way to conceptualize the level of student involvement in learning is the Cone of Experience, designed originally by Edgar Dale in 1969. The handout "Learning Activities" (page 100) is inspired by Dale's (1969) work and provides a pyramid of possible learning activities. It aims to help teachers select instructional practices that truly engage students in the learning process—so that students don't just receive the knowledge passively but see how it functions in real life by doing something meaningful with it. Do note that we have changed the original model from percentages to relative terms (*little*, *less*, *more*, and so on) to potentially be more accurate, since specific percentages may not be based on true empirical evidence of how much students learn from various modalities.

The handout "Planning for Student Active Learning" (page 101) encourages teachers to plan a lesson by considering the tiers of learning activities and levels of student engagement. If teachers think of their teaching time as 100 percent, how do they allocate it to the listed categories of student activities? Is the time allocation optimal for achieving learning goals?

Self-Assessment of Active Learning

	Very Frequently	Frequently	Occasionally	Rarely	Never
Authenticity					
I think about my learning within authentic contexts and reflect on ways the knowledge will be tangible and useful in real life.					
I understand that problems in real life are sometimes fuzzy and not well defined, so I aspire to emulate what experts would do and seek out multiple sources and perspectives.					
Sense of Agency					
I ask questions for clarification.					
I sustain a positive and enthusiastic attitude about learning.					
I extend my learning with additional reading, discussions with others about what we learned, and applications of learning.					
Collaboration					
I discuss what I learned with others in order to validate my ability to clearly articulate what I think I know.					
I exchange views, share research findings, and debate topics with others.					
Higher-Order Thinking					
I politely challenge ideas, procedures, content connections, and priorities.					
I connect what I most recently learned with what I previously learned.					
I have an open mind—instead of making snap judgments, I use reasoning skills and support my claims with solid arguments.					

Instructional Methods for Differentiation and Deeper Learning © 2016 Solution Tree Press • solution-tree.com

Visit **go.solution-tree.com/instruction** to download this page.

	Very Frequently	Frequently	Occasionally	Rarely	Never
Monitoring					
I continuously assess the quality of my learning throughout the major task.					
I reflect on my learning, both individually and as part of a team.					

Source: Adapted from Grabinger, R. S., & Dunlap, J. C. (1995). Rich environments for active learning: A definition. Association for Learning Technology Journal, 3(2), 5–34.

Learning Activities

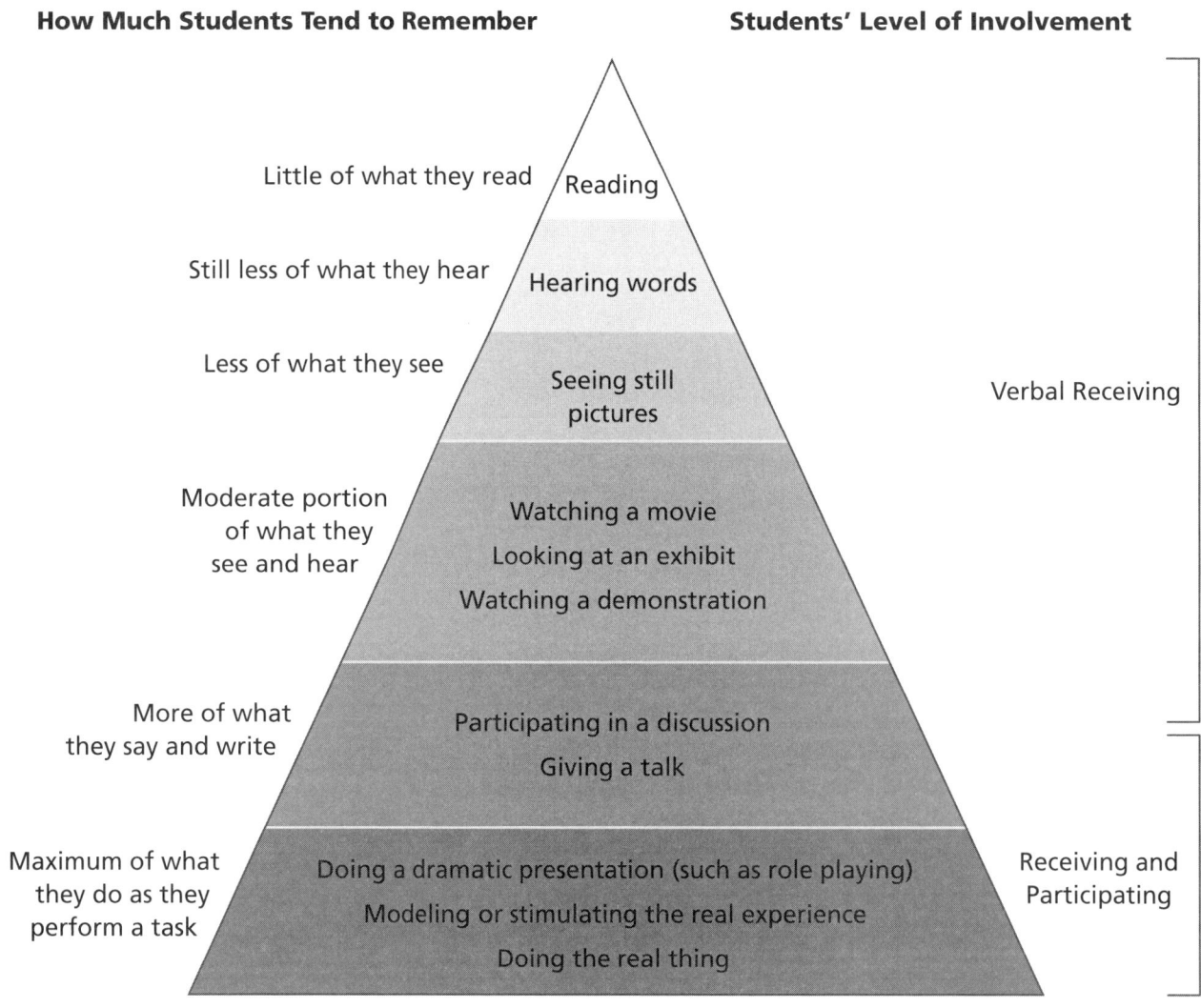

Planning for Student Active Learning

Identify the specific learning activities you will use.

Circle the expected learning outcomes.

____% Reading

____% Listening

____% Seeing

____% Seeing and listening

Define	Recall
Recognize	Locate
Describe	List
Explain	Paraphrase
Summarize	State
Repeat	Memorize
Label	Duplicate

Other: _____

____% Saying and writing

____% Doing and performing

Demonstrate	Apply
Illustrate	Employ
Practice	Analyze
Design	Create
Evaluate	Show

Other: _____

As you are planning for the lesson, please consider the following questions.
- Where will the learning activities fit on the learning activities cone?
- How far is the learning activity removed from active learning?
- How do the instructional materials augment active learning?

Chapter 10
Problem-Based Learning

The Gallup Corporation, in collaboration with Microsoft Partners in Learning and the Pearson Foundation, developed a 21st century skill index measuring seven specific areas (Levy & Sidhu, 2013): (1) collaboration, (2) knowledge construction, (3) skilled communication, (4) global awareness, (5) self-regulation, (6) real-world problem solving, and (7) technology use in learning. The findings indicate that of all these seven areas, real-world problem solving is most strongly linked to self-reported work success. However, only 29 percent of the surveyed young adults (aged eighteen to thirty-five) say they learned to develop solutions to real-world problems in school (Levy & Sidhu, 2013).

Schools and classrooms have a significant effect on students' long-term work quality when teachers integrate real-world problem solving into the curriculum. The workplace increasingly calls for skills in effectively analyzing and resolving issues. Consequently, teachers may need to renew—or in some cases, reinvent—classroom instruction to help students learn to build and integrate deeper understanding, become autonomous learners and thinkers, and explore and solve important, real problems.

Problem-based learning is one way teachers can help students find and apply knowledge to solve real-world problems. The complexity of today's society demands that learners be successful problem solvers who not only have a deep and well-organized knowledge base but also possess the skills to apply this knowledge to solve problems in an efficient way (Dochy, Segers, Van den Bossche, & Gijbels, 2003).

Problem-based learning uses authentic, real-life problems to engage students in learning that has personal meaning for them. Howard Barrows (1996) outlines six core characteristics of problem-based learning.

1. Learning is student centered.
2. Learning occurs in small groups.
3. The teacher acts as a facilitator or guide.
4. The teacher presents authentic problems at the beginning of the learning sequence.
5. Teachers use the problems that students encounter as tools to help them achieve the required knowledge and the problem-solving skills necessary to eventually solve the problems.
6. Students acquire new information through self-directed learning.

With problem-based learning, students not only have rich opportunities to acquire subject-matter knowledge, but also—and perhaps, more importantly—they develop and practice the thinking and application skills they need to put knowledge to work.

What Research Says About Problem-Based Learning

Much of the initial research on problem-based learning was restricted to higher education, since the approach was originally developed for medical school education in the late 1960s (Hmelo-Silver, 2004; Walker & Leary, 2009). However, since 2000, researchers have conducted a plethora of studies within K–12 schools comparing the effectiveness of problem-based learning and conventional instructional approaches. For instance, a study by Leman

Tarhan and Burcin Acar-Sesen (2013) finds that when compared with a teacher-centered approach, students in a problem-based learning group have higher achievement in understanding chemistry content and more positive beliefs toward the subject. Alfred Fatade, Abayomi Arigbabu, David Mogari, and Adeneye Awofala (2014) also report a positive impact on students' beliefs about mathematics stemming from problem-based learning.

A quasi-experimental study finds that problem-based learning could support the development of data literacy for middle school students (*data literacy* refers to the ability to ask and answer meaningful questions by collecting, analyzing, and making sense of data encountered in everyday lives) (Swan, Vahey, van 't Hooft, Kratcoski, & Rafanan, 2013). Similarly, Jennifer Yeo and Seng Chee Tan (2014) find that problem-based learning can promote middle school students' achievement with the dual goal of learning science content and developing problem-solving skills. John Hattie (2009) demonstrates that problem-based learning has an average effect size of 0.61 on student learning outcomes. In summary, problem-based learning, especially in skill development, can be a powerful learning tool.

How to Move From Research to Practice

Problem-based learning is organized around the identification, investigation, and resolution of meaningful problems. Students work collaboratively in small groups of around five to ten students to discover and define the problem, develop hypotheses to explain the problem, and explore preexisting knowledge relating to the problem. They assess what they already know regarding the problem and what they need to research in order to increase their knowledge about the problem (Mennin, Gordan, Majoor, & Osman, 2003).

First of all, the teacher presents students with a problem scenario. The problem serves as an important initiator for cognitive conflict or puzzlement and determines the nature of learning (Savery & Duffy, 2001). Researchers suggest that an ideal problem needs to have the following characteristics (Hmelo-Silver, 2004; Sockalingam & Schmidt, 2013).

- **Complex:** The problem should be complex enough to provide students the opportunity to evaluate the effectiveness of their knowledge, reasoning, and learning strategies.
- **Open ended:** The problem should promote conjecture and argumentation.
- **Multidisciplinary:** This encourages students to practice skills from various subjects and integrate their understanding of concepts across disciplines.
- **Contextualized:** The problem should include background information so students can internalize it and gain motivation to know and learn more about it.
- **Authentic:** The problem should be realistic and relevant to the students' experience, and it should represent the kind of challenges that students will encounter in real life.
- **Built on prior knowledge:** The problem should be designed to fit with students' prior knowledge and experiences so they can identify with the learning.

Once teachers expose them to a problem scenario, students formulate and analyze the problem by identifying the relevant facts. This step helps students dissect and represent the problem. They also are better able to organize their ideas and connect with previous knowledge as they decipher the problem. As students understand the problem better, they generate hypotheses about possible solutions.

Students then begin identifying knowledge deficiencies relative to the problem, otherwise known as the topics that students need to investigate in order to resolve it. They collectively decide which of the learning issues they will research and then create an action plan. Next, students engage in a self-directed phase of learning to gather, analyze, evaluate, and synthesize the new knowledge. To do so, they must learn to locate and evaluate information from books, journals, library databases, and other online information resources. This phase allows the students to personalize their learning as they pursue topics of interest and concentrate on areas of knowledge deficiency.

Then students apply their new knowledge and evaluate their hypotheses in light of what they have learned. At this phase, students share with one another what they have learned from their individual research. Within groups, they compare, discuss, and debate as they begin to integrate the new knowledge to solve the problem. Teachers identify and assign new learning issues as students go progressively deeper with their learning. The process continues until the group reaches a consensus on a resolution to the problem. At the completion of the problem, students reflect on the abstract knowledge they gained. The teacher helps students reflect on the skills they used for problem solving and collaboration (Hmelo-Silver, 2004). Figure 10.1 represents the major steps in the cycle of problem-based learning.

In problem-based learning, students actively decide what concepts and principles they should understand better and where to get the information they need in order to resolve the problems. Teachers expect them to own their learning and self-direct their progress and also hold students responsible for the learning of others in the group.

The Teacher's Role in Problem-Based Learning

Problem-based learning is a major form of student-centered learning, but student-centered learning does not mean that the teacher lets go of all the control and direction. In fact, there is little empirical evidence to suggest that experientially based, unguided study can foster high-quality learning. Rather, the research related to problem-based learning generally supports scaffolding with the teacher as a guide as essential for the success of problem-based learning (Hmelo-Silver, Duncan, & Chinn, 2007; Kirschner, Sweller, & Richard, 2006; Wijnia, Loyens, van Gog, Derous, & Schmidt, 2014).

Given the importance of guidance, students do not learn entirely on their own in problem-based learning situations. The teacher still teaches, but the timing and extent of the instructional interventions differ from those used in traditional teacher-directed approaches. In terms of timing, the teacher may wait for teachable moments before intervening or providing necessary content explanations (such as when students need clarification or recognize that they must learn something new).

Essentially, teachers actively guide the processes of learning. They take a facilitative role, answering questions, moving groups along, monitoring positive and negative behavior, and watching for opportunities to direct students to specific resources or to provide clarifying explanations (Mergendoller, Maxwell, & Bellisimo, 2006). Furthermore, teachers guide discovery and analysis; provide constructive feedback; ask questions to scaffold and stimulate student thinking; ensure that student-directed learning reaches set standards for developing scope of knowledge, reasoning ability, and communication skills; and focus on building skills for self- and peer assessment (Mennin et al., 2003).

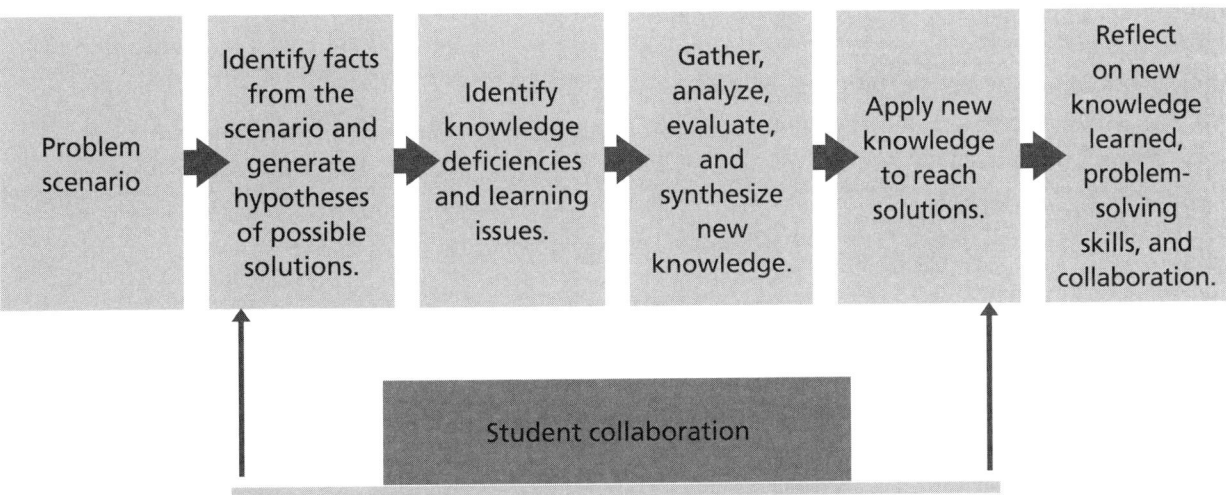

Figure 10.1: The problem-based learning cycle.

The learning environment is a dichotomy of acquisition versus participation (Yeo & Tan, 2014). Acquisition-based learning assumes that knowledge is objective and external and can transfer to learners as receivers of knowledge. Teacher-directed learning is a typical example of this learning style. Participation-based learning is based on the situated nature of knowledge. It assumes that learning is a social process of participation in a community. Learners do not focus on learning about the subject content; instead, they approach learning like professionals in a discipline. The research we have shared indicates that problem-based learning is more effective for learning problem-solving skills than content learning. Therefore, we recommend that teachers aim for a facilitative role promoting a balance of acquisition and participation, because students need to be able to solve problems in particular contexts but also must achieve deep learning of knowledge that they can generalize to future situations.

A Case Study

To illustrate once again what we referred to in chapter 8 (problem-based learning indeed involves complex thinking), let's consider the example of Anson High School in Wadesboro, North Carolina (Vander Ark & Schneider, 2014). The teachers at Anson believe problem solving begins by identifying an authentic, genuine issue of importance in the world and then working to solve it. They teach as teams across the boundaries of disciplines and involve students in service learning to solve real community problems. For instance, the students have programmed a metal fabrication robot welder, created an entire light and sound system for the local arts council, and updated old computers for a local preK program. By integrating real problems into the curriculum and having students work on solving them, the students develop positive academic attitudes and a sense of belonging within a community of learners. The students also see themselves as achievers and develop confidence by demonstrating competence.

Summary

Problem-based learning involves whole units focused on complex and realistic problems. It requires a complete rethinking of the roles of teacher and students in the classroom. Rather than being the dispenser of knowledge, teachers guide students to be skillful thinkers and inquirers. And instead of passively receiving knowledge, students actively investigate, construct understanding, and build a meaningful scaffold where they can "hang" the knowledge. We've put together a collection of handouts to help teachers use problem-based learning in their classrooms.

Within problem-based learning, the teacher becomes more of a facilitator of knowledge rather than the dominant content expert. Nonetheless, the teacher still actively guides learning experiences. One important strategy to facilitate student learning in any context (not just in problem-based learning) is scaffolding. Scaffolding provides the incentive for students to actively participate in their own learning. The idea is very similar to Lev Vygotsky's (1978) theory on the zone of proximal development. The handout "Teacher Scaffolding" summarizes a number of scaffolding techniques that teachers can tap into.

The handout "Process Worksheet" (page 109) captures the major steps in problem-based learning. Students can use it to guide a problem-based learning process.

Problem-based learning is characterized by authentic, student-centered learning with the teacher acting as facilitator. The handout "Teacher Self-Assessment Checklist" (page 111) presents the key tenets and purposes of problem-based learning; teachers can use it to assess whether they have accomplished the goals of problem-based learning.

Teacher Scaffolding

Scaffolding Technique	Should I Use This Technique?
Anchor the learning activities to real-life, authentic problems, and make the connections clear.	☐ Yes ☐ No Comment:
Model or demonstrate how to perform a new or difficult task.	☐ Yes ☐ No Comment:
Use advance organizers to introduce new content and tasks (such as a Venn diagram to compare and contrast, a flow chart to illustrate process, rubrics to clarify expectations, an organizational chart to illustrate hierarchies, or outlines to summarize key themes).	☐ Yes ☐ No Comment:
Use examples (such as samples or illustrations) to represent a concept or phenomenon.	☐ Yes ☐ No Comment:
Provide more detailed explanations to move students along on a task or in their thinking.	☐ Yes ☐ No Comment:
Provide handouts that have structural information for a larger picture but room for student notes.	☐ Yes ☐ No Comment:
Provide suggestions and hints to redirect students in their thinking (such as "Why don't you try . . . ?").	☐ Yes ☐ No Comment:
Provide cue cards to assist students in their discussion about a particular topic or content area (such as key vocabulary, content-specific stem sentences to complete, model, template, steps, formula, or concepts to define).	☐ Yes ☐ No Comment:
Ask probing questions for students to recall prior knowledge, make connections, or think from a different point of view.	☐ Yes ☐ No Comment:
Assess prerequisite skills that students need in order to be successful on the new task, and reteach if needed.	☐ Yes ☐ No Comment:

Scaffolding Technique	Should I Use This Technique?
Ask questions to prompt students to manage their investigation and problem-solving process and to encourage them to articulate and reflect on their thinking.	☐ Yes ☐ No Comment:
Adjust the learning activities to make them more manageable.	☐ Yes ☐ No Comment:
Provide informative and constructive feedback.	☐ Yes ☐ No Comment:
Encourage testing ideas against alternative views and alternative contexts.	☐ Yes ☐ No Comment:

Sources: Adapted from Faculty Development and Instructional Design Center, Northern Illinois University. (2008). Instructional scaffolding to improve learning. TA Connections Newsletter. *Accessed at www.niu.edu/taconnections/2008/fall/scaffolding.shtml on October 21, 2014; Hmelo-Silver, C. E. (2004). Problem-based learning: What and how do students learn?* Educational Psychology Review, *16(3), 235–266.*

Process Worksheet

Use the questions under each header as prompts for your thinking.

Problem

How do I internalize the problem?

How is the problem relevant to my real-life experience?

Facts

What do I already know about the problem?

How can I synthesize the information I have to support my hypotheses?

What are my conjectures regarding the problem, such as hypotheses regarding the causation, effect, and possible resolution?

Learning Issues

What do I need to know or understand in order to complete the problem task?

What key issues should I focus my efforts on?

Action Plans

What are the specific steps I need to take to gather appropriate resources?

What information or tasks will I analyze, synthesize, and evaluate to resolve the problem?

Apply New Knowledge

If I apply my new knowledge to the problem, how do my hypotheses stand in light of what I have just learned?

Which solution do I choose? Why?

Teacher Self-Assessment Checklist

	Accomplished	Not Accomplished
The problem-based learning resulted in better content knowledge.		
The problem-based learning resulted in better conceptual knowledge.		
The problem-based learning resulted in better problem-solving skills.		
The problem-based learning resulted in better metacognitive skills.		
The problem-based learning resulted in better attitudes toward learning.		
The problem-based learning resulted in better communication and teamwork skills.		
The problem-based learning resulted in better skills in applying learning to solve problems.		
I anchored all learning activities to a larger authentic problem.		
I gave students ownership of the process to develop a solution.		
I structured the tasks and learning environment in a way to reflect the complexity of the real-life environment in which students should be able to function.		
I established a positive learning environment to support and challenge student thinking.		
I gave students opportunities and support for reflection on both the content learned and the learning process.		

Self-reflections:

References and Resources

Aghaie, R., & Zhang, L. J. (2012). Effects of explicit instruction in cognitive and metacognitive reading strategies on Iranian EFL students' reading performance and strategy transfer. *Instructional Science, 40*(6), 1063–1081.

Aljughaiman, A., & Mowrer-Reynolds, E. (2005). Teachers' conceptions of creativity and creative students. *Journal of Creative Behavior, 39*(1), 17–34.

American Institutes for Research. (2014). *Deeper learning.* Accessed at www.air.org/resource/deeper-learning on July 13, 2015.

Anderson, L. W., & Krathwohl, D. R. (Eds.). (2001). *A taxonomy for learning, teaching, and assessing: A revision of Bloom's taxonomy of educational objectives* (Complete ed.). New York: Longman.

Angelo, T. A., & Cross, K. P. (1993). *Classroom assessment techniques: A handbook for college teachers* (2nd ed.). San Francisco: Jossey-Bass.

Archambault, F. X., Jr., Westberg, K. L., Brown, S. W., Hallmark, B. W., Zhang, W., & Emmons, C. L. (1993). Classroom practices used with gifted third and fourth grade students. *Journal for the Education of the Gifted, 16*(2), 103–119.

Archambault, I., Janosz, M., Fallu, J.-S., & Pagani, L. S. (2009). Student engagement and its relationship with early high school dropout. *Journal of Adolescence, 32*(3), 651–670.

Askell-Williams, H., Lawson, M. J., & Skrzypiec, G. (2012). Scaffolding cognitive and metacognitive strategy instruction in regular class lessons. *Instructional Science, 40*(2), 413–443.

Au, K. H. (2009). Culturally responsive instruction: What is it, and how can we incorporate it in the classroom? *Reading Today, 27*(3), 30–31.

Azzam, A. M. (2009). Why creativity now? A conversation with Sir Ken Robinson. *Educational Leadership, 67*(1), 22–26.

Baartman, L. K. J., & de Bruijn, E. (2011). Integrating knowledge, skills and attitudes: Conceptualising learning processes towards vocational competence. *Educational Research Review, 6*(2), 125–134.

Baepler, P., Walker, J. D., & Driessen, M. (2014). It's not about seat time: Blending, flipping, and efficiency in active learning classrooms. *Computers and Education, 78,* 227–236.

Bambrick-Santoyo, P. (2010). *Driven by data: A practical guide to improve instruction.* San Francisco: Jossey-Bass.

Bang, M., & Medin, D. (2010). Cultural processes in science education: Supporting the navigation of multiple epistemologies. *Science Education, 94*(6), 1008–1026.

Barrows, H. S. (1986). A taxonomy of problem-based learning methods. *Medical Education, 20*(6), 481–486.

Barrows, H. S. (1996). Problem-based learning in medicine and beyond. In L. Wilkerson & W. H. Gijselaers (Eds.), *Bringing problem-based learning to higher education: Theory and practice* (pp. 3–13). San Francisco: Jossey-Bass.

Beghetto, R. A. (2007). Ideational code-switching: Walking the talk about supporting student creativity in the classroom. *Roeper Review, 29*(4), 265–270.

Beghetto, R. A., & Kaufman, J. C. (2013). Fundamentals of creativity. *Educational Leadership, 70*(5), 10–15.

Blaas, S. (2014). The relationship between social-emotional difficulties and underachievement of gifted students. *Australian Journal of Guidance & Counselling, 24*(2), 243–255.

Blackburn, B. R. (2013). *Rigor is not a four-letter word* (2nd ed.). New York: Routledge.

Bloom, B. S. (1984). The 2 sigma problem: The search for methods of group instruction as effective as one-to-one tutoring. *Educational Researcher, 13*(6), 4–16.

Bloom, D. S., & Peters, T. (2012). Student teaching experience in diverse settings: White racial identity development and teacher efficacy. *Journal of Educational and Developmental Psychology, 2*(2), 72–84.

Borders, C., Woodley, S., & Moore, E. (2014). Inclusion and giftedness. *Advances in Special Education, 26,* 127–146.

Borich, G. D. (1988). *Effective teaching methods.* Columbus, OH: Merrill.

Borich, G. D. (2011). *Effective teaching methods: Research-based practice* (7th ed.). Boston: Pearson.

Boylan, H. R., & Saxon, D. P. (1999). *What works in remediation: Lessons from 30 years of research.* Accessed at http://inpathways.net/Boylan--What%20Works.pdf on March 3, 2015.

Bronson, P., & Merryman, A. (2010, July 10). The creativity crisis. *Newsweek.* Accessed at www.newsweek.com/2010/07/10/the-creativity-crisis.html on March 3, 2015.

Brophy, J., & Good, T. L. (1986). Teacher behavior and student achievement. In M. C. Wittrock (Ed.), *Handbook of research on teaching* (3rd ed., pp. 328–371). New York: Macmillan.

Brown-Jeffy, S., & Cooper, J. (2011). Toward a conceptual framework of culturally relevant pedagogy: An overview of the conceptual and theoretical literature. *Teacher Education Quarterly, 38*(1), 65–84.

Cachia, R., & Ferrari, A. (2010). *Creativity in schools: A survey of teachers in Europe.* Seville, Spain: European Commission, Joint Research Centre, Institute for Prospective Technological Studies.

Callahan, C. M., Moon, T. R., Oh, S., Azano, A. P., & Hailey, E. P. (2015). What works in gifted education: Documenting the effects of an integrated curricular/instructional model for gifted students. *American Educational Research Journal, 52*(1), 137–167.

Carjuzaa, J., & Ruff, W. G. (2010). When western epistemology and an indigenous worldview meet: Culturally responsive assessment in practice. *Journal of the Scholarship of Teaching and Learning, 10*(1), 68–79.

Cawelti, G. (Ed.). (2004). *Handbook of research on improving student achievement* (3rd ed.). Arlington, VA: Educational Research Service.

Center for Excellence in Learning and Teaching. (n.d.). *Techniques for creative teaching.* Accessed at www.celt.iastate.edu/teaching-resources/classroom-practice/teaching-techniques-strategies/creativity/techniques-creative-teaching on October 6, 2014.

Chan, Y.-Y., Hui, D., Dickinson, A. R., Chu, D., Cheng, D. K.-W., Cheung, E., et al. (2010). Engineering outreach: A successful initiative with gifted students in science and technology in Hong Kong. *IEEE Transactions on Education, 53*(1), 158–171.

Changeiywo, J. M., Wambugu, P. W., & Wachanga, S. W. (2011). Investigations of students' motivation towards learning secondary school physics through mastery learning approach. *International Journal of Science and Mathematics Education, 9*(6), 1333–1350.

Cheesman, E., & De Pry, R. (2010). A critical review of culturally responsive literacy instruction. *Journal of Praxis in Multicultural Education, 5*(1), 83–99.

Cheng, Y.-Y., Wang, W.-C., Liu, K.-S., & Chen, Y.-L. (2010). Effects of association instruction on fourth graders' poetic creativity in Taiwan. *Creativity Research Journal, 22*(2), 228–235.

Chung, C.-C., Dzan, W.-Y., Shih, R.-C., Tsai, H.-Y., & Lou, S.-J. (2012). Creativity learning through blended teaching for designing amphibious vehicles. *International Journal of Technology and Engineering Education, 9*(1), 33–43.

Clifford, M. M. (1990). Students need challenge, not easy success. *Educational Leadership, 48*(1), 22–26.

Coiro, J. (2011). Talking about reading as thinking: Modeling the hidden complexities of online reading comprehension. *Theory Into Practice, 50*(2), 107–115.

Collins, A., Brown, J. S., & Holum, A. (1991). Cognitive apprenticeship: Making thinking visible. *American Educator, 15*(3), 6–11, 38–46.

Comas-Diaz, L. (2000). An ethnopolitical approach to working with people of color. *American Psychologist, 55*(11), 1319–1325.

Cotton, K. (1989). *Expectations and student outcomes.* Accessed at http://educationnorthwest.org/sites/default/files/ExpectationsandStudentOutcomes.pdf on July 29, 2015.

Covino, E. A., & Iwanicki, E. F. (1996). Experienced teachers: Their constructs of effective teaching. *Journal of Personnel Evaluation in Education, 10*(4), 325–363.

Crawford, A., Saul, W., Mathews, S. R., & Makinster, J. (2005). *Teaching and learning strategies for the thinking classroom.* New York: International Debate Education Association.

Critical Thinking Community. (n.d.). *Defining critical thinking.* Accessed at www.criticalthinking.org/pages/defining-critical-thinking/766 on March 3, 2015.

Cropley, A. J. (2001). *Creativity in education and learning: A guide for teachers and educators.* Philadelphia: Kogan Page.

Crumpton, H. E. (2011). "I'm not learning": The role of academic relevancy for low-achieving students. *Journal of Educational Research, 104*(1), 42–53.

Csikszentmihalyi, M., Rathunde, K., & Whalen, S. (1993). *Talented teenagers: The roots of success and failure.* New York: Cambridge University Press.

Dabarera, C., Renandya, W. A., & Zhang, L. J. (2014). The impact of metacognitive scaffolding and monitoring on reading comprehension. *System, 42*, 462–473.

Dale, E. (1969). *Audiovisual methods in teaching* (3rd ed.). New York: Dryden Press.

Daly, E. J., III, Witt, J. C., Martens, B. K., & Dool, E. J. (1997). A model for conducting a functional analysis of academic performance problems. *School Psychology Review, 26*(4), 554–574.

Davidman, L., & Davidman, P. T. (2001). *Teaching with a multicultural perspective: A practical guide* (3rd ed.). New York: Longman.

de Bono for Schools. (2015). *Six thinking hats: A tool to strengthen critical thinking, collaboration, communication, and creativity skills.* Accessed at www.debonoforschools.com/asp/six_hats.asp on July 15, 2015.

DeLoach, S. B., & Greenlaw, S. A. (2005). Do electronic discussions create critical thinking spillovers? *Contemporary Economic Policy, 23*(1), 149–163.

Deruy, E. (2013, March 21). *Student diversity is up but teachers are mostly white.* Accessed at https://aacte.org/news-room/aacte-in-the-news/347-student-diversity-is-up-but-teachers-are-mostly-white on November 2, 2014.

Dikici, A. (2014). Relationships between thinking styles and behaviors fostering creativity: An exploratory study for the mediating role of certain demographic traits. *Educational Sciences: Theory and Practice, 14*(1), 179–201.

Dochy, F., Segers, M., Van den Bossche, P., & Gijbels, D. (2003). Effects of problem-based learning: A meta-analysis. *Learning and Instruction, 13*(5), 533–568.

Dolezal, S. E., Welsh, L. M., Pressley, M., & Vincent, M. M. (2003). How nine third-grade teachers motivate student academic engagement. *Elementary School Journal, 103,* 239–267.

Dunn, R., & Dunn, K. (1992). *Teaching elementary students through their individual learning styles: Practical approaches for grades 3–6.* Boston: Allyn & Bacon.

Dunn, R., & Honigsfeld, A. (2009). *Differentiating instruction for at-risk students: What to do and how to do it.* Lanham, MD: Rowman & Littlefield.

Edmonds, M. S., Vaughn, S., Wexler, J., Reutebuch, C., Cable, A., Tackett, K. K., et al. (2009). A synthesis of reading interventions and effects on reading comprehension outcomes for older struggling readers. *Review of Educational Research, 79*(1), 262–300.

Elbaum, B., Vaughn, S., Hughes, S. V., & Moody, S. W. (2000). How effective are one-to-one tutoring programs in reading for elementary students at risk for reading failure? A meta-analysis of the intervention research. *Journal of Education Psychology, 92*(4), 605–618.

Elder, L., & Paul, R. (1996). Critical thinking: A stage theory of critical thinking. *Journal of Developmental Education, 20*(1), 34–35.

Ennis, R. H. (2000a, October 18). *An outline of goals for critical thinking curriculum and its assessment.* Accessed at www.criticalthinking.net/goals.html on March 3, 2015.

Ennis, R. H. (2000b). *Teaching critical thinking: A few suggestions.* Accessed at www.criticalthinking.net/teaching.html on October 17, 2014.

Epstein, T., Mayorga, E., & Nelson, J. (2011). Teaching about race in an urban history class: The effects of culturally responsive teaching. *Journal of Social Studies Research, 35*(1), 2–21.

Esquivel, G. B. (1995). Teacher behaviors that foster creativity. *Educational Psychology Review, 7*(2), 185–202.

Faculty Development and Instructional Design Center, Northern Illinois University. (2008). Instructional scaffolding to improve learning. *TA Connections Newsletter.* Accessed at www.niu.edu/taconnections/2008/fall/scaffolding.shtml on October 21, 2014.

Fatade, A. O., Arigbabu, A. A., Mogari, D., & Awofala, A. O. A. (2014). Investigating senior secondary school students' beliefs about further mathematics in a problem-based learning context. *Bulgarian Journal of Science and Education Policy, 8*(1), 5–46.

Ferguson, R. F. (1998). Teachers' perceptions and expectations and the Black-White test score gap. In C. Jencks and M. Phillips (Eds.), *The black-white test score gap.* Washington, DC: Brookings Institution Press.

Finegold, D., & Notabartolo, A. S. (2010). *21st-century competencies and their impact: An interdisciplinary literature review.* Accessed at www.hewlett.org/uploads/21st_Century_Competencies_Impact.pdf on March 3, 2015.

Fleith, D. D. (2000). Teacher and student perceptions of creativity in the classroom environment. *Roeper Review, 22*(3), 148–153.

French, L. R., Walker, C. L., & Shore, B. M. (2011). Do gifted students really prefer to work alone? *Roeper Review, 33*(3), 145–159.

Fuchs, L. S., Powell, S. R., Seethaler, P. M., Cirino, P. T., Fletcher, J. M., Fuchs, D., et al. (2009). Remediating number combination and word problem deficits among students with mathematics difficulties: A randomized control trial. *Journal of Educational Psychology, 101*(3), 561–576.

Fullan, M., & Langworthy, M. (2013). *Towards a new end: New pedagogies for deep learning.* Seattle, WA: Collaborative Impact.

Gallagher, J. J. (2005). Commentary: National security and educational excellence. *Education Week, 24*(38), 32–33, 40.

Gallagher, S. A., Stepien, W. J., & Rosenthal, H. (1992). The effects of problem-based learning on problem solving. *Gifted Child Quarterly, 36*(4), 195–200.

Garcia, E. E. (1991). *The education of linguistically and culturally diverse students: Effective instructional practices* (Educational Practice Report 1). Washington, DC: National Center for Research on Cultural Diversity and Second Language Learning. Accessed at http://escholarship.org/uc/item/2793n11s on March 3, 2015.

Gay, G. (2000). *Culturally responsive teaching: Theory, research, and practice.* New York: Teachers College Press.

Gerard, J. G., Knott, M. J., & Lederman, R. E. (2012). Three examples using tablet technology in an active learning classroom: Strategies for active learning course design using tablet technology. *Global Education Journal, 2012*(4), 91–114.

GettingSmart. (2014). *Anson New Technology High School: Leaders of the pack.* Accessed at http://gettingsmart.com/wp-content/uploads/2014/01/FINAL-Anson-New-Tech_Final-Designed1.pdf on July 16, 2015.

Gijbels, D., Dochy, F., Van den Bossche, P., & Segers, M. (2005). Effects of problem-based learning: A meta-analysis from the angle of assessment. *Review of Educational Research, 75*(1), 27–61.

Göçmençelebi, Ş. İ., Özkan, M., & Bayram, N. (2012). Evaluating primary school students' deep learning approach to science lessons. *International Online Journal of Educational Sciences, 4*(3), 554–562.

Gong, R. (2005). The essence of critical thinking. *Journal of Developmental Education, 28*(3), 40.

Gonzalez, V., Brusca-Vega, R., & Yawkey, T. (1997). *Assessment and instruction of culturally and linguistically diverse students with or at-risk of learning problems: From research to practice.* Boston: Allyn & Bacon.

Good, T. L., & Brophy, J. E. (2007). *Looking in classrooms* (10th ed.). Boston: Allyn & Bacon.

Gordon, E. E. (2009). 5 ways to improve tutoring programs: Evidence on tutoring points to practices that are found in the most successful tutoring programs. *Phi Delta Kappan, 90,* 440–445.

Gorski, P. C., Davis, S. N., & Reiter, A. (2012). Self-efficacy and multicultural teacher education in the United States: The factors that influence who feels qualified to be a multicultural teacher educator. *Multicultural Perspectives, 14*(4), 220–228.

Gouthro, P. A., & Holloway, S. M. (2013). Preparing teachers to become lifelong learners: Exploring the use of fiction to develop multiliteracies and critical thinking. *Language and Literacy: A Canadian Educational E-Journal, 15*(3), 50–68.

Grabinger, R. S., & Dunlap, J. C. (1995). Rich environments for active learning: A definition. *Association for Learning Technology Journal, 3*(2), 5–34.

Graffam, B. (2006). A case study of teachers of gifted learners: Moving from prescribed practice to described practitioners. *Gifted Child Quarterly, 50*(2), 119–131.

Green, G. P., Bean, J. C., & Peterson, D. J. (2013). Deep learning in intermediate microeconomics: Using scaffolding assignments to teach theory and promote transfer. *Journal of Economic Education, 44*(2), 142–157.

Greene, B., & Cross, T. L. (2013). Setting the bar for high-ability students. *Principal Leadership, 14*(2), 46–49.

Greene, B. A., Miller, R. B., Crowson, H. M., Duke, B. L., & Akey, K. L. (2004). Predicting high school students' cognitive engagement and achievement: Contributions of classroom perceptions and motivation. *Contemporary Educational Psychology, 29*(4), 462–482.

Greenlaw, S. A., & DeLoach, S. B. (2003). Teaching critical thinking with electronic discussion. *Journal of Economic Education, 34*(1), 36–52.

Guo, S.-J., Tsai, C.-H., Chang, F. M.-T., & Huang, H.-I. (2007). The study of questioning skills on teaching improvement. *International Journal of Learning, 14*(8), 141–145.

Halpern, D. F. (1998). Teaching critical thinking for transfer across domains: Dispositions, skills, structure training, and metacognitive monitoring. *American Psychologist, 53*(4), 449–455.

Harmin, M. (2006). *Inspiring active learning: A complete handbook for today's teachers* (2nd ed.). Alexandria, VA: Association for Supervision and Curriculum Development.

Harris, C. M., & Zha, S. (2013). Concept mapping: A critical thinking technique. *Education, 134*(2), 207–211.

Hartman, H. J. (Ed.). (2001). *Metacognition in learning and instruction: Theory, research and practice*. Norwell, MA: Kluwer.

Hasan, S. S., & Khalid, R. (2014). Academic locus of control of high and low achieving students. *Journal of Research & Reflections in Education, 8*(1), 22–33.

Hattie, J. (2009). *Visible learning: A synthesis of over 800 meta-analyses relating to achievement*. New York: Routledge.

Hiebert, J., Stigler, J. W., Jacobs, J. K., Givvin, K. B., Garnier, H., Smith, M., et al. (2005). Mathematics teaching in the United States today (and tomorrow): Results from the TIMSS 1999 video study. *Educational Evaluation and Policy Analysis, 27*(2), 111–132.

Hidalgo, F., Chávez-Chávez, R., & Ramage, J. (1996). Multicultural education: Landscape for reform in the twenty-first century. In J. Sikula, T. Buttery, & E. Guyton (Eds.), *Handbook of research on teacher education* (2nd ed., pp. 761–778). New York: Macmillan.

Hmelo-Silver, C. E. (2004). Problem-based learning: What and how do students learn? *Educational Psychology Review, 16*(3), 235–266.

Hmelo-Silver, C. E., Duncan, R. G., & Chinn, C. A. (2007). Scaffolding and achievement in problem-based and inquiry learning: A response to Kirschner, Sweller, and Clark (2006). *Educational Psychologist, 42*(2), 99–107.

Holt, L. C., & Kysilka, M. (2006). *Instructional patterns: Strategies for maximizing student learning*. Thousand Oaks, CA: SAGE.

Huberman, M., Bitter, C., Anthony, J., & O'Day, J. (2014). *The shape of deeper learning: Strategies, structures, and cultures in deeper learning network high schools—Findings from the study of deeper learning opportunities and outcomes* (Report 1). Washington, DC: American Institutes for Research.

Hughes, G. K., Cowley, K. S., Copley, L. D., Finch, N. L., Meehan, M. L., Burns, R. C., et al. (2004). *Effects of a culturally responsive teaching project on teachers and students in selected Kanawha County, WV, schools*. Charleston, WV: AEL.

Ibata-Arens, K. C. (2012). Race to the future: Innovations in gifted and enrichment education in Asia, and implications for the United States. *Administrative Sciences, 2*(1), 1–25.

Intel Teach Program. (2007). *Designing effective projects: Questioning—The Socratic questioning technique*. Accessed at www.intel.com/content/dam/www/program/education/us/en/documents/project-design/strategies/dep-question-socratic.pdf on September 17, 2014.

İskifoğlu, G. (2014). Cross-cultural equivalency of the California critical thinking disposition inventory. *Educational Sciences: Theory and Practice, 14*(1), 159–178.

Jeffrey, B. (2006). Creative teaching and learning: Towards a common discourse and practice. *Cambridge Journal of Education, 36*(3), 399–414.

Jeffrey, B., & Craft, A. (2004). Teaching creatively and teaching for creativity: Distinctions and relationships. *Educational Studies, 30*(1), 77–87.

Johnsen, S. K., & Ryser, G. R. (1996). An overview of effective practices with gifted students in general-education settings. *Journal for the Education of the Gifted, 19*(4), 379–404.

Kanevsky, L. (2011). Deferential differentiation: What types of differentiation do students want? *Gifted Child Quarterly, 55*(4), 279–299.

Kelly, S., & Carbonaro, W. (2012). Curriculum tracking and teacher expectations: Evidence from discrepant course taking models. *School Psychology of Education, 15*(3), 271–294.

Kim, K. H. (2011). The creativity crisis: The decrease in creative thinking scores on the Torrance tests of creative thinking. *Creativity Research Journal, 23*(4), 285–295.

Kipper, H., & Rüütmann, T. (2010). Strategies and techniques of questioning effectuating thinking and deep understanding in teaching engineering at Estonian Centre for Engineering Pedagogy. *Problems of Education in the 21st Century, 19*, 36–45.

Kirschner, P. A., Sweller, J., & Richard, R. E. (2006). Why minimal guidance during instruction does not work: An analysis of the failure of constructivist, discovery, problem-based, experiential, and inquiry-based teaching. *Educational Psychologist, 41*(2), 75–86.

Knapp, M. S., Shields, P. M., & Turnbull, B. J. (1995). Academic challenge in high-poverty classrooms. *Phi Delta Kappan, 76*(10), 770–776.

Koedinger, K. R., Booth, J. L., & Klahr, D. (2013). Instructional complexity and the science to constrain it. *Science, 342*(6161), 935–937.

Köksal, O., Yagisan, N., & Aksoy, Y. (2013). The impact of active learning activities on attainment, attitudes and retention in secondary school students in music lessons. *Journal of Education and Sociology, 4*(2), 89–98.

Kong, S. C. (2014). Developing information literacy and critical thinking skills through domain knowledge learning in digital classrooms: An experience of practicing flipped classroom strategy. *Computers and Education, 78*, 160–173.

Konstantopoulos, S., Modi, M., & Hedges, L. V. (2001). Who are America's gifted? *American Journal of Education, 109*(3), 344–382.

Kramarski, B., Mevarech, Z. R., & Arami, M. (2002). The effects of metacognitive instruction on solving mathematical authentic tasks. *Educational Studies in Mathematics, 49*(2), 225–250.

Kuh, G. (2003). What we're learning about engagement from NSSE. *Change, 35*(2), 24–32.

Kysilka, M. L., & Biraimah, K. (1993). *The thinking teacher: Ideas for effective learning* (2nd ed.). New York: McGraw-Hill.

Lai, E. R. (2011). *Critical thinking: A literature review* [Research report]. Accessed at http://images.pearson assessments.com/images/tmrs/CriticalThinkingReviewFINAL.pdf on July 15, 2015.

Leary, H., Walker, A., Shelton, B. E., & Fitt, M. H. (2013). Exploring the relationships between tutor background, tutor training, and student learning: A problem-based learning meta-analysis. *Interdisciplinary Journal of Problem-Based Learning, 7*(1), 39–66.

Lee, N. H., Yeo, D. J. S., & Hong, S. E. (2014). A metacognitive-based instruction for Primary Four students to approach non-routine mathematical word problems. *ZDM Mathematics Education, 46*(3), 465–480.

Lee, S.-Y., Olszewski-Kubilius, P., & Peternel, G. (2010). The efficacy of academic acceleration for gifted minority students. *Gifted Child Quarterly, 54*(3), 189–208.

Levy, J., & Sidhu, P. (2013, May 30). *In the U.S., 21st century skills linked to work success: Real-world problem-solving most strongly tied to work quality*. Accessed at www.gallup.com/poll/162818/21st-century-skills-linked-work-success.aspx on March 3, 2015.

Limbrick, L., Wheldall, K., & Madelaine, A. (2012). Do boys need different remedial reading instruction from girls? *Australian Journal of Learning Difficulties*, *17*(1), 1–15.

Lin, C.-H., Liu, E. Z.-F., Chen, Y.-L., Liou, P.-Y., Chang, M., Wu, C.-H., et al. (2013). Game-based remedial instruction in mastery learning for upper-primary school students. *Educational Technology and Society*, *16*(2), 271–281.

Lipman, M. (1991). *Thinking in education.* Cambridge, England: Cambridge University Press.

Liu, S.-C., & Lin, H.-S. (2014). Primary teachers' beliefs about scientific creativity in the classroom context. *International Journal of Science Education*, *36*(10), 1551–1567.

Loveless, T., Farkas, S., & Duffett, A. (2008). *High-achieving students in the era of NCLB.* Washington, DC: Thomas B. Fordham Institute.

Martin, R., Sexton, C., & Franklin, T. (2005). *Teaching science for all children: Inquiry methods for constructing understanding* (3rd ed.). Boston: Allyn & Bacon.

Marzano, R. J., Pickering, D. J., & Pollock, J. E. (2001). *Classroom instruction that works: Research-based strategies for increasing student achievement.* Alexandria, VA: Association for Supervision and Curriculum Development.

Mason, D. A., Schroeter, D. D., Combs, R. K., & Washington, K. (1992). Assigning average-achieving eighth graders to advanced mathematics classes in an urban junior high. *Elementary School Journal*, *92*(5), 587–599.

Matsko, V., & Thomas, J. (2014). The problem is the solution: Creating original problems in gifted mathematics classes. *Journal for the Education of the Gifted*, *37*(2), 153–170.

Matthews, M. S., Ritchotte, J. A., & McBee, M. T. (2013). Effects of schoolwide cluster grouping and within-class ability grouping on elementary school students' academic achievement growth. *High Ability Studies*, *24*(2), 81–97.

McAllister, G., & Irvine, J. J. (2008). Cross cultural competency and multicultural teacher education. In C. A. Grant & T. K. Chapman (Eds.), *History of multicultural education: Teachers and teacher education* (Vol. 6, pp. 63–82). New York: Routledge.

McDermott, P. A., & Watkins, M. W. (1983). Computerized vs. conventional remedial instruction for learning-disabled pupils. *Journal of Special Education*, *17*(1), 81–88.

Mennin, S., Gordan, P., Majoor, G., & Osman, H. A. (2003). Position paper on problem-based learning. *Education for Health*, *16*(1), 98–113.

Mergendoller, J. R., Maxwell, N. L., & Bellisimo, Y. (2006). The effectiveness of problem-based instruction: A comparative study of instructional methods and student characteristics. *Interdisciplinary Journal of Problem-Based Learning*, *1*(2), 49–69.

Metacognition. (n.d.). In *Wikipedia*. Accessed at http://en.wikipedia.org/wiki/Metacognition on September 17, 2014.

Metcalfe, J., & Shimamura, A. P. (Eds.). (1994). *Metacognition: Knowing about knowing.* Cambridge, MA: MIT Press.

Mevarech, Z. R., & Kramarski, B. (1997). IMPROVE: A multidimensional method for teaching mathematics in heterogeneous classrooms. *American Educational Research Journal*, *34*(2), 365–394.

Meyer, D. K., Turner, J. C., & Spencer, C. A. (1997). Challenge in a mathematics classroom: Students' motivation and strategies in project-based learning. *Elementary School Journal*, *97*(5), 501–521.

Michalsky, T., Mevarech, Z. R., & Haibi, L. (2009). Elementary school children reading scientific texts: Effects of metacognitive instruction. *Journal of Educational Research*, *102*(5), 363–376.

Mills, C. J. (2003). Characteristics of effective teachers of gifted students: Teacher background and personality styles of students. *Gifted Child Quarterly*, *47*(4), 272–281.

Morrison-Shetlar, A., & Marwitz, M. (2001). *Teaching creatively: Ideas in action.* Eden Prairie, MN: Outernet.

Nadelson, L. S., Boham, M. D., Conlon-Khan, L., Fuentealba, M. J., Hall, C. J., Hoetker, G. A., et al. (2012). A shifting paradigm: Preservice teachers' multicultural attitudes and efficacy. *Urban Education, 47*(6), 1183–1208.

National Governors Association Center for Best Practices & Council of Chief State School Officers. (2010a). *Common Core State Standards for English language arts and literacy in history/social studies, science, and technical subjects.* Washington, DC: Authors. Accessed at www.corestandards.org/assets/CCSSI_ELA%20 Standards.pdf on April 17, 2015.

National Governors Association Center for Best Practices & Council of Chief State School Officers. (2010b). *Common Core State Standards for mathematics.* Washington, DC: Authors. Accessed at www.corestandards .org/assets/CCSSI_Math%20Standards.pdf on April 20, 2015.

National Research Council. (2012). *Education for life and work: Developing transferable knowledge and skills in the 21st century.* Washington, DC: National Academies Press.

National Society for the Gifted and Talented. (2015). *Giftedness defined.* Accessed at www.nsgt.org/giftedness -defined on July 9, 2015.

Nussbaum, E. M. (2005). The effect of goal instructions and need for cognition on interactive argumentation. *Contemporary Educational Psychology, 30*(3), 286–313.

Odabaşi, B., & Kolburan, G. (2013). Employment of active learning in classroom management and its effect on students' academic success. *Journal of Education and Sociology, 4*(2), 21–25.

Organisation for Economic Co-operation and Development. (2009). *Education at a glance 2009: OECD indicators.* Accessed at www.oecd.org/edu/skills-beyond-school/educationataglance2009oecdindicators.htm on July 9, 2015.

Organisation for Economic Co-operation and Development. (2012). *Results from PISA 2012: United States* [Country note]. Accessed at www.oecd.org/unitedstates/PISA-2012-results-US.pdf on October 31, 2014.

Organisation for Economic Co-operation and Development. (2014). *PISA 2012 results in focus: What 15-year-olds know and what they can do with what they know.* Paris: Author.

Orlich, D. C., Harder, R. J., Callahan, R. C., & Gibson, H. W. (2001). *Teaching strategies: A guide to better instruction* (6th ed.). Boston: Houghton Mifflin.

Osborn, J., Freeman, A., Burley, M., Wilson, R., Jones, E., & Rychener, S. (2007). Effect of tutoring on reading achievement for students with cognitive disabilities, specific learning disabilities, and students receiving Title I services. *Education and Training in Developmental Disabilities, 42*(4), 467–474.

Pellegrino, J. W., & Hilton, M. L. (Eds.). (2012). *Education for life and work: Developing transferable knowledge and skills in the 21st century.* Washington, DC: National Academies Press.

Peregoy, S. F., & Boyle, O. F. (2000). English learners reading English: What we know, what we need to know. *Theory Into Practice, 39*(4), 237–247.

Petress, K. (2008). What is meant by "active learning"? *Education, 128*(4), 566–569.

Pierce, R. L., Cassady, J. C., Adams, C. M., Neumeister, K. L. S., Dixon, F. A., & Cross, T. L. (2011). The effects of clustering and curriculum on the development of gifted learners' math achievement. *Journal for the Education of the Gifted, 34*(4), 569–594.

Polette, N. (2005). *Teaching thinking skills with fairy tales and fantasy.* Westport, CT: Teacher Ideas Press.

Polleck, J., & Shabdin, S. (2013). Building culturally responsive communities. *The Clearing House, 86,* 142–149.

Powell, J., & Stansell, A. (2014, June 23). Cognitive apprenticeship through problem-based learning. In J. Herrington, J. Viteli, & M. Leikomaa (Eds.), *EdMedia World Conference on Educational Media and Technology 2014* (pp. 2256–2261). Chesapeake, VA: Association for the Advancement of Computing in Education.

Prince, M. (2004). Does active learning work? A review of the research. *Journal of Engineering Education*, *93*(3), 223–231.

Question. (n.d.). In *Merriam-Webster's online dictionary*. Accessed at www.merriam-webster.com/dictionary/question on September 17, 2014.

Reinfried, S., Aeschbacher, U., & Rottermann, B. (2012). Improving students' conceptual understanding of the greenhouse effect using theory-based learning materials that promote deep learning. *International Research in Geographical and Environmental Education*, *21*(2), 155–178.

Reinsvold, L. A., & Cochran, K. F. (2012). Power dynamics and questioning in elementary science classrooms. *Journal of Science Teacher Education*, *23*(7), 745–768.

Reis, S. M., McCoach, D. B., Little, C. A., Muller, L. M., & Kaniskan, R. B. (2011). The effects of differentiated instruction and enrichment pedagogy on reading achievement in five elementary schools. *American Educational Research Journal*, *48*(2), 462–501.

Revell, A., & Wainwright, E. (2009). What makes lectures 'unmissable'? Insights into teaching excellence and active learning. *Journal of Geography in Higher Education*, *33*(2), 209–223.

Robinson, A., Dailey, D., Hughes, G., & Cotabish, A. (2014). The effects of a science-focused STEM intervention on gifted elementary students' science knowledge and skills. *Journal of Advanced Academics*, *25*(3), 189–213.

Robinson, A., Shore, B. M., & Enersen, D. L. (2007). *Best practices in gifted education: An evidence-based guide*. Waco, TX: Prufrock Press.

Robinson, K. (2006). *Do schools kill creativity?* Accessed at www.ted.com/talks/ken_robinson_says_schools_kill_creativity?language=en on July 15, 2015.

Rogers, K. B. (2007). Lessons learned about educating the gifted and talented: A synthesis of the research on educational practice. *Gifted Child Quarterly*, *51*(4), 382–396.

Rogers-Chapman, F., & Darling-Hammond, L. (2013). *Preparing 21st century citizens: The role of work-based learning in linked learning*. Stanford, CA: Stanford Center for Opportunity Policy in Education.

Rosen, Y., & Tager, M. (2014). Making student thinking visible through a concept map in computer-based assessment of critical thinking. *Journal of Educational Computing Research*, *50*(2), 249–270.

Rubenstein, L. D., McCoach, D. B., & Siegle, D. (2013). Teaching for creativity scales: An instrument to examine teachers' perceptions of factors that allow for the teaching of creativity. *Creativity Research Journal*, *25*(3), 324–334.

Rubie-Davies, C. M. (2006). Teacher expectations and student self-perceptions: Exploring relationships. *Psychology in the Schools*, *43*(5), 537–552.

Rubie-Davies, C. M., Flint, A., & McDonald, L. G. (2012). Teacher beliefs, teacher characteristics, and school contextual factors: What are the relationships? *British Journal of Educational Psychology*, *82*, 270–288.

Runco, M. A., Millar, G., Acar, S., & Cramond, B. (2010). Torrance tests of creative thinking as predictors of personal and public achievement: A fifty-year follow-up. *Creativity Research Journal*, *22*(4), 361–368.

Rychly, L., & Graves, E. (2012). Teacher characteristics for culturally responsive pedagogy. *Multicultural Perspectives*, *14*(1), 44–49.

Saine, N. L., Lerkkanen, M.-K., Ahonen, T., Tolvanen, A., & Lyytinen, H. (2010). Predicting word-level reading fluency outcomes in three contrastive groups: Remedial and computer-assisted remedial reading intervention, and mainstream instruction. *Learning and Individual Differences*, *20*(5), 402–414.

Sakiz, G., Pape, S. J., & Hoy, A. W. (2012). Does perceived teacher affective support matter for middle school students in mathematics classrooms? *Journal of School Psychology*, *50*(2), 235–255.

Sanders, W. L., & Horn, S. P. (1998). Research findings from the Tennessee Value-Added Assessment System (TVAAS) database: Implications for educational evaluation and research. *Journal of Personnel Evaluation in Education, 12*(3), 247–256.

Savery, J. R., & Duffy, T. M. (2001). *Problem based learning: An instructional model and its constructivist framework* (Technical Report No. 16-01). Bloomington, IN: Center for Research on Learning and Technology.

Shernoff, D. J., Csikszentmihalyi, M., Schneider, B., & Shernoff, E. S. (2003). Student engagement in high school classrooms from the perspective of flow theory. *School Psychology Quarterly, 18*(2), 158–176.

Silberman, M. (1996). *Active learning: 101 strategies to teach any subject.* Boston: Allyn & Bacon.

Slavin, R. E., & Madden, N. A. (1989). What works for students at risk: A research synthesis. *Educational Leadership, 46*(5), 4–13.

Smith, D. G. (1977). College classroom interactions and critical thinking. *Journal of Educational Psychology, 69*(2), 180–190.

Sockalingam, N., & Schmidt, H. G. (2013). Does the extent of problem familiarity influence students' learning in problem-based learning? *Instructional Science, 41*(5), 921–932.

Sorhagen, N. S. (2013). Early teacher expectations disproportionately affect poor children's high school performance. *Journal of Educational Psychology, 105*(2), 465–477.

Sousa, D. A., & Tomlinson, C. A. (2011). *Differentiation and the brain: How neuroscience supports the learner-friendly classroom.* Bloomington, IN: Solution Tree Press.

Stahl, R. J. (1994). *Using "think-time" and "wait-time" skillfully in the classroom* (ERIC Digest). Bloomington, IN: ERIC Clearinghouse for Social Studies/Social Science Education. (ED370885)

Starko, A. J. (2005). *Creativity in the classroom: Schools of curious delight* (3rd ed.). Mahwah, NJ: Erlbaum.

Starko, A. J. (2013). Creativity on the brink? *Educational Leadership, 70*(5), 54–56.

Steenbergen-Hu, S., & Moon, S. M. (2011). The effects of acceleration on high-ability learners: A meta-analysis. *Gifted Child Quarterly, 55*(1), 39–53.

Sternberg, R. J. (1998). Metacognition, abilities, and developing expertise: What makes an expert student? *Instructional Science, 26*(1–2), 127–140.

Sternberg, R. J. (2003). What is an "expert student"? *Educational Researcher, 32*(8), 5–9.

Sternberg, R. J., & Williams, W. M. (1996). *How to develop student creativity.* Alexandria, VA: Association for Supervision and Curriculum Development.

Stronge, J. H. (2007). *Qualities of effective teachers* (2nd ed.). Alexandria, VA: Association for Supervision and Curriculum Development.

Stronge, J. H., Grant, L., & Xu, X. (2015). Teachers and teaching. In J. D. Wright (Ed.), *International encyclopedia of the social and behavioral sciences* (2nd ed., pp. 44–50). Maryland Heights, MO: Elsevier.

Stronge, J. H., Little, C. A., & Grant, L. W. (2009). Qualities of talented teachers: Reflections and new directions. In B. MacFarlane & T. Stambaugh (Eds.), *Leading change in gifted education: The festschrift of Dr. Joyce VanTassel-Baska* (pp. 389–401). Waco, TX: Prufrock Press.

Stronge, J. H., Ward, T. J., Tucker, P. D., & Hindman, J. L. (2007). What is the relationship between teacher quality and student achievement? An exploratory study. *Journal of Personnel Evaluation in Education, 20*(3–4), 165–184.

Stronge, J. H., & Xu, X. (2016). *Instructional strategies for effective teaching.* Bloomington, IN: Solution Tree Press.

Swan, K., Vahey, P., van 't Hooft, M., Kratcoski, A., & Rafanan, K. (2013). Problem-based learning across the curriculum: Exploring the efficacy of a cross-curricular application of preparation for future learning. *Interdisciplinary Journal of Problem-Based Learning*, *7*(1), 89–110.

Tarhan, L., & Acar-Sesen, B. (2013). Problem based learning in acids and bases: Learning achievements and students' beliefs. *Journal of Baltic Science Education*, *12*(5), 565–578.

Tawfik, A., Trueman, R. J., & Lorz, M. M. (2014). Engaging non-scientists in STEM through problem-based learning and service learning. *Interdisciplinary Journal of Problem-Based Learning*, *8*(2), 76–84.

Taylor, B. M., Pearson, P. D., Clark, K. F., & Walpole, S. (1999). Effective schools/accomplished teachers. *The Reading Teacher*, *53*(2), 156–159.

Taylor, B. M., Pearson, P. D., Peterson, D. S., & Rodriguez, M. C. (2003). Reading growth in high-poverty classrooms: The influence of teacher practices that encourage cognitive engagement in literacy learning. *Elementary School Journal*, *104*(1), 3–28.

Teaching Center, Washington University in St. Louis. (2009). *Asking questions to improve learning.* Accessed at http://teachingcenter.wustl.edu/strategies/Pages/asking-questions.aspx on March 3, 2015.

Thomas, G. P. (2003). Conceptualization, development and validation of an instrument for investigating the metacognitive orientation of science classroom learning environments: The Metacognitive Orientation Learning Environment Scale—Science (MOLES-S). *Learning Environments Research*, *6*, 175–197.

Tobin, K. G. (1980). The effect of an extended teacher wait-time on science achievement. *Journal of Research in Science Teaching*, *17*(5), 469–475.

Tobin, K. G., & Capie, W. (1982). Relationships between classroom process variables and middle-school science achievement. *Journal of Educational Psychology*, *74*(3), 441–454.

Tobin, R., & Tippett, C. D. (2014). Possibilities and potential barriers: Learning to plan for differentiated instruction in elementary science. *International Journal of Science and Mathematics Education*, *12*(2), 423–443.

Tomlinson, C. A. (2003). *Fulfilling the promise of the differentiated classroom: Strategies and tools for responsive teaching.* Alexandria, VA: Association of Supervision and Curriculum Development.

Tomlinson, C. A., & Imbeau, M. B. (2010). *Leading and managing a differentiated classroom.* Alexandria, VA: Association for Supervision and Curriculum Development.

Tsui, L. (1999). Courses and instruction affecting critical thinking. *Research in Higher Education*, *40*(2), 185–200.

Tsui, L. (2002). Fostering critical thinking through effective pedagogy: Evidence from four institutional case studies. *Journal of Higher Education*, *73*(6), 740–763.

University of Michigan. (n.d.). *The six types of Socratic questions.* Accessed at www.umich.edu/~elements/probsolv/strategy/cthinking.htm on September 17, 2014.

U.S. Department of Labor. (2010). *2010–11 editions of the Occupational Outlook Handbook and the Career Guide to Industries news release.* Accessed at www.bls.gov/news.release/archives/ooh_12172009.htm on July 30, 2015.

Vaish, V. (2013). Questioning and oracy in a reading program. *Language and Education*, *27*(6), 526–541.

van den Bergh, L., Ros, A., & Beijaard, D. (2013). Teacher feedback during active learning: Current practices in primary schools. *British Journal of Educational Psychology*, *83*(2), 341–362.

Vander Ark, T., & Schneider, C. (2014). *Deeper learning for every student every day.* Accessed at www.hewlett.org/sites/default/files/Deeper%20Learning%20for%20Every%20Student%20EVery%20Day_GETTING%20SMART_1.2014.pdf on July 16, 2015.

VanGundy, A. B. (2005). *101 activities for teaching creativity and problem solving.* San Francisco: Pfeiffer.

VanTassel-Baska, J. (2003). *Curriculum planning and instructional design for gifted learners.* Denver, CO: Love.

VanTassel-Baska, J. (2011). An introduction to the integrated curriculum model. In J. VanTassel-Baska & C. A. Little (Eds.), *Content-based curriculum for high-ability learners* (2nd ed., pp. 9–32). Waco, TX: Prufrock Press.

VanTassel-Baska, J. (2014). Curriculum issues: Artful inquiry—The use of questions in working with the gifted. *Gifted Child Today, 37*(1), 48–50.

VanTassel-Baska, J., & Brown, E. F. (2007). Toward best practice: An analysis of the efficacy of curriculum models in gifted education. *Gifted Child Quarterly, 51*(4), 342–358.

VanTassel-Baska, J., & Little, C. A. (Eds.). (2011). *Content-based curriculum for high-ability learners* (2nd ed.). Waco, TX: Prufrock Press.

Vogler, K. E. (2008). Asking good questions. *Educational Leadership, 65*(9). Accessed at www.ascd.org/publications/educational-leadership/summer08/vol65/num09/Asking-Good-Questions.aspx on July 30, 2015.

Vygotsky, L. S. (1978). *Mind in society: The development of higher mental processes.* Cambridge, MA: Harvard University Press.

Wagner, T. (2008a). *The global achievement gap: Why even our best schools don't teach the new survival skills our children need—and what we can do about it.* New York: Basic Books.

Wagner, T. (2008b). Rigor redefined. *Educational Leadership, 66*(2), 20–25.

Walker, A., & Leary, H. (2009). A problem based learning meta analysis: Differences across problem types, implementation types, disciplines, and assessment levels. *Interdisciplinary Journal of Problem-Based Learning, 3*(1), 6–28.

Walsh, J. A., & Sattes, B. D. (2005). *Quality questioning: Research-based practice to engage every learner.* Thousand Oaks, CA: Corwin Press.

Wambugu, P. W., & Changeiywo, J. M. (2008). Effects of mastery learning approach on secondary school students' physics achievement. *Eurasia Journal of Mathematics, Science and Technology Education, 4*(3), 293–302.

Warren, S. R. (2002). Stories from the classrooms: How expectations and efficacy of diverse teachers affect the academic performance of children in poor urban schools. *Educational Horizons, 80*(3), 109–116.

Watkins, R. (2005). *75 e-learning activities: Making online learning interactive.* San Francisco: Pfeiffer.

Wenglinsky, H. (2004). Closing the racial achievement gap: The role of reforming instructional practices. *Education Policy Analysis Archives, 12*(64), 1–22. Accessed at http://epaa.asu.edu/ojs/article/download/219/345 on October 29, 2014.

Westberg, K. L., Archambault, F. X., Jr., Dobyns, S. M., & Salvin, T. J. (1993). *An observational study of instructional and curricular practices used with gifted and talented students in regular classrooms* (Research Monograph No. 93104). Storrs, CT: National Research Center on the Gifted and Talented, University of Connecticut.

Westberg, K. L., & Daoust, M. E. (2003, Fall). The results of the replication of the Classroom Practices Survey replication in two states. *National Research Center on the Gifted and Talented Newsletter.* Accessed at www.gifted.uconn.edu/nrcgt/newsletter/fall03/fall032.html on January 4, 2010.

Westby, E. L., & Dawson, V. L. (1995). Creativity: Asset or burden in the classroom? *Creativity Research Journal, 8*(1), 1–10.

Weinstein, C. S., Tomlinson-Clarke, S., & Curran, M. (2004). Toward a conception of culturally responsive classroom management. *Journal of Teacher Education, 55*(1), 25–38.

Wijnia, L., Loyens, S. M. M., van Gog, T., Derous, E., & Schmidt, H. G. (2014). Is there a role for direct instruction in problem-based learning? Comparing student-constructed versus integrated model answers. *Learning and Instruction, 34*, 22–31.

William and Flora Hewlett Foundation. (2013, April). *Deeper learning competencies.* Accessed at www.hewlett.org/uploads/documents/Deeper_Learning_Defined__April_2013.pdf on March 3, 2015.

Wright, S. P., Horn, S. P., & Sanders, W. L. (1997). Teacher and classroom context effects on student achievement: Implications for teacher evaluation. *Journal of Personnel Evaluation in Education, 11*(1), 57–67.

Yee, K. (n.d.). *Interactive techniques.* Accessed at www.fctl.ucf.edu/TeachingAndLearningResources/CourseDesign/Assessment/content/101_Tips.pdf on March 3, 2015.

Yeo, J., & Tan, S. C. (2014). Redesigning problem-based learning in the knowledge creation paradigm for school science learning. *Instructional Science, 42*(5), 747–775.

Zahorik, J., Halbach, A., Ehrle, K., & Molnar, A. (2003). Teaching practices for smaller classes. *Educational Leadership, 61*(1), 75–77.

Zhao, Y. (2009). *Catching up or leading the way: American education in the age of globalization.* Alexandria, VA: Association for Supervision and Curriculum Development.

Zhao, Y. (2012). *World class learners: Educating creative and entrepreneurial students.* Thousand Oaks, CA: Corwin Press.

Zohar, A., & Barzilai, S. (2013). A review of research on metacognition in science education: Current and future directions. *Studies in Science Education, 49*(2), 121–169.

Zohar, A., & Peled, B. (2008). The effects of explicit teaching of metastrategic knowledge on low- and high-achieving students. *Learning and Instruction, 18*(4), 337–353.

Index

A

Acar-Sesen, B., 104
active learning
    defined, 93
    feedback, 94
    group and pair work, 96
    individual work, 95–96
    learner and teacher attributes for, 94
    learning activities, 97, 100
    lectures, 95
    multimedia, use of, 96–97
    planning, 97, 101
    research on, 94
    self-assessment, 97, 98–99
    strategies for implementing, 94–97
    teacher-centered instruction versus, 94, 95
    teaching attributes that promote, 93
Ahonen, T., 9
American Institutes for Research, 35
Archambault, F., 18–19
Arigbabu, A., 104
Askell-Williams, H., 51
Au, K. H., 27–28
Awofala, A., 104

B

Bambrick-Santoyo, P., 12, 13–14
Bang, M., 28
Barrows, H., 103
blogs, 97
Bloom, D., 28
Bloom's mastery learning, 8
Bloom's revised taxonomy, 40, 41
Booth, J., 85
Boylan, H., 8, 10–11
Brophy, J., 85, 86–87

C

Callahan, R., 69
Chang, F. M.-T., 39

Chávez-Chávez, R., 27
Clifford, M., 84
coaching, 71
cognitive apprenticeship, 70–71
Common Core State Standards, gifted students and, 18
complex thinking
    ABC list, 85, 89
    affects of student input, 82
    checklist on the depth of instruction, 85, 86–87
    defined, 81
    dimensions and domains of, 83–84
    example of, 83–84
    research on, 81–83
    strategies for implementing, 84
    strategy reflection activity, 85, 88
    teacher self-assessment, 85, 90–91
computer-assisted instruction, 9
Cone of Experience (Dale), 97
creativity
    characteristics, 60–61
    critical thinking versus creative thinking, 60
    guidelines for fostering, 61–62
    measuring, 62, 68
    process for promoting, 62, 64–67
    research on, 59–60
    self-assessment, 62, 63
    teaching for, versus teaching creatively, 59
critical thinking
    checklist, 74, 79
    defined, 69
    framework, 72
    process and stages of, 72
    questions that make students mindful, 73, 75–77
    research on, 70–71
    skills, 73
    strategies for implementing, 71–73
    student self-assessment, 74, 78
Critical Thinking Community, 69–70
Cropley, A., 21–22, 24–25, 61

culturally and linguistically diverse students
    growth and impact of, 27
    implementation of programs and instruction for, 29–30
    prerequisites for helping, 29
    research on, 28
    student learning profile, 31, 34
    teacher reflection, 30, 32
culturally responsive instruction
    characteristics of, 31, 33
    defined, 27–28
culturally responsive teacher, framework for, 27

D

Dale, E., 97, 100
Daly, E., 11
data literacy, 104
deeper learning
    defined, 35
    role of, 1–2
DeLoach, S., 74, 79
differentiated instruction
    benefits of, 1
    lesson plan, 21, 23
    See also culturally and linguistically diverse students; gifted students
differentiated remedial instruction
    defined, 7
    effect sizes, 7–8
    implementation of, 9–11
    instructional strategies, 11
    learning style model, 12, 15
    research on, 7–9
    role of, 7
    student survey, 12, 16
    weaknesses in student learning, identifying, 12, 13–14
diverse learners. *See* culturally and linguistically diverse students
Dool, E., 11
"Do Schools Kill Creativity?" (Robinson), 62
Dunlap, J., 93, 97
Dunn, R., 12, 15

E

Elder, L., 72
Enersen, D., 22
Ennis, R., 71
Epstein, T., 28
equity, 21
Esquivel, G., 59
Evidence-Centered Concept Map, 70
excellence, 21

F

fading, 71
Fatade, A., 104
feedback
    active learning and, 94
    questioning and, 40
Fleith, D. D., 60
flow theory, 81–82
Fuchs, L. S., 8

G

Gallagher, J., 21
Gallup Corporation, 103
Garcia, E., 28
Gay, G., 31, 33
Gibson, H., 69
gifted students
    Common Core State Standards and, 18
    defined, 17–18
    lesson plan, differentiation, 21, 23
    research on, 18–19
    research-supported practices for, 22, 26
    self-assessment checklist, 21–22, 24–25
    strategies to use with, 19–21
Gong, R., 73–74
Good, T., 85, 86–87
Grabinger, R. S., 93, 97
Graffam, B., 18
Greenlaw, S., 74, 79
Guo, S.-J., 39

H

Halpern, D., 73
Harder, R., 69
Hartman, H., 51
Hattie, J., 104
Hewlett Foundation, 83
Hidalgo, F., 27
Holt, L., 60
Huang, H.-I., 39
Huberman, M., 82

I

Irvine, J. J., 28

J

Jeffrey, B., 60–61
Johnsen, S., 20–21

K

Klahr, D., 85
Koedinger, K., 85
Köksal, O., 94
Kolburan, G., 94
Kong, S. C., 70, 72
Kuh, G., 10
Kysilka, M., 60

L

Lawson, M., 51
learning style model, 12, 15
lectures, 95
Lerkkanen, M.-K., 9
lesson plan, differentiation, 21, 23
Limbrick, L., 8
Lin, C.-H., 9
Lipman, M., 73
low expectations, effects of, 9–10
Lyytinen, H., 9

M

Madden, N., 7, 8, 10
Madelaine, A., 8
Martens, B., 11
mastery learning, 8
Mayorga, E., 28
McAllister, G., 28
McDermott, P., 8
Medin, D., 28
metacognition
    defined, 51
    example of, 53–55
    research on, 51–52
    self-assessment, 55, 56–58
    strategies for developing, 52–53
metastrategic knowledge, 52
Microsoft Partners in Learning, 103
modeling, 70
Mogari, D., 104

multimedia, use of, 96–97

N

Nadelson, L., 28
National Research Council, 84
Nelson, J., 28

O

Odabaşi, B., 94
Orlich, D., 69, 71

P

Paul, R., 72
Pearson Foundation, 103
Peled, B., 52
Peters, T., 28
problem-based learning
    characteristics, 103
    cycle, 105
    effect size, 104
    example of, 106
    process worksheet, 106, 109–110
    research on, 103–104
    scaffolding, 106, 107–108
    strategies for implementing, 104–105
    teacher self-assessment, 106, 111
    teacher's role in, 105–106
Programme for International Student Assessment (PISA), 17, 82

Q

questioning
    checklist, 41, 45
    closed-ended, 37
    content-focused, design form, 42–43, 49
    factual and procedural, 37–38
    feedback, 40
    for learning domains, 41, 46–47
    metacognitive, 57
    mindful, 73, 75–77
    open-ended, 37
    openness, 39
    purposes, types, and levels of, 40, 41, 42
    research on, 37–39
    role of, 37
    Socratic, 42
    speculative and process, 38

student-developed, 42, 48
technique analysis, 40–41, 44
trends in classroom, 38
wait time, 39

R

Ramage, J., 27
remedial instruction. *See* differentiated remedial instruction
Revell, A., 95
Robinson, A., 22
Robinson, K., 62
Rosen, Y., 69, 70
Rubie-Davies, C., 10
Ryser, G., 20–21

S

Saine, N., 9
Sattes, B., 38, 39
Saxon, D. P., 8, 10–11
scaffolding, 71, 84, 106, 107–108
self-assessment
    active learning, 97, 98–99
    checklist, 21–22, 24–25
    complex thinking, 85, 90–91
    creativity, 62, 63
    critical thinking, 74, 78
    metacognition, 55, 56–58
    problem-based learning, 106, 111
self-fulfilling prophecy, 10
Shore, B., 22
Skrzypiec, G., 51
Slavin, R., 7, 8, 10
Smith, D., 70
Socratic questions, 42
Sousa, D., 21
STEM, 28
Sternberg, R., 2, 53
student-developed questioning, 42, 48
student learning profile, 31, 34
student self-assessment, critical thinking and, 74, 78
student survey, 12, 16

T

Tager, M., 69, 70
Tan, S. C., 104
Tarhan, L., 103–104
Taylor, B., 82
teacher-centered instruction versus active learning, 94, 95
teacher reflection, 30, 32
teacher self-assessment
    of complex thinking, 85, 90–91
    of metacognition, 55, 58
    of problem-based learning, 106, 111
Third International Mathematics and Science Study (TIMSS), 81
Thomas, G., 51
Tolvanen, A., 9
Tomlinson, C. A., 21
Torrance, E. P., 62
Tsai, C.-H., 39
Tsui, L., 70
tutoring, 8–9
21st century skill index, 103
Twitter, 96

V

Van Tassel-Baska, J., 19–20
Vygotsky, L., 106

W

Wagner, T., 1
Wainwright, E., 95
Walsh, J., 38, 39
Watkins, M., 8
"What Makes a Lecture 'Unmissable'?" (Revell and Wainwright), 95
Wheldall, K., 8
wikis, 96–97
Witt, J., 11

Y

Yeo, J., 104
YouTube, 96

Z

Zhao, Y., 59
Zohar, A., 52
zone of proximal development, 106

Unstoppable Learning
Douglas Fisher and Nancy Frey
Discover how systems thinking can enhance teaching and learning schoolwide. Examine how to use systems thinking—which involves distinguishing patterns and considering short- and long-term consequences—to better understand the big picture of education and the intricate relationships that impact classrooms.
BKF662

The Five Dimensions of Engaged Teaching
Laura Weaver and Mark Wilding
Engaged teaching recognizes that educators need to offer more than lesson plans and assessments for students to thrive in the 21st century. Equip your students to be resilient individuals, able to communicate effectively and work with diverse people.
BKF601

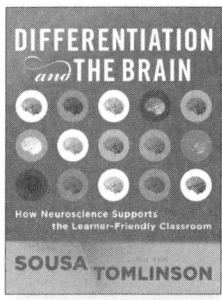

Differentiation and the Brain
David A. Sousa and Carol Ann Tomlinson
Examine the basic principles of differentiation in light of educational neuroscience research that will help you make the most effective curricular, instructional, and assessment choices. Learn how to implement differentiation so that it achieves the desired result of shared responsibility between teacher and student.
BKF353

Deeper Learning
James A. Bellanca
Education authorities from around the globe draw on research as well as their own experience to explore deeper learning, a process that promotes higher-order thinking, reasoning, and problem solving to better educate students and prepare them for college and careers.
BKF622

Mind, Brain, & Education
David A. Sousa
Understanding how the brain learns helps teachers do their jobs more effectively. Primary researchers in the emerging field of educational neuroscience share the latest findings on the learning process and address their implications for educational theory and practice.
BKF358

Visit solution-tree.com or call 800.733.6786 to order.

Wait! Your professional development journey doesn't have to end with the last pages of this book.

We realize improving student learning doesn't happen overnight. And your school or district shouldn't be left to puzzle out all the details of this process alone.

No matter where you are on the journey, we're committed to helping you get to the next stage.

Take advantage of everything from **custom workshops** to **keynote presentations** and **interactive web and video conferencing**. We can even help you develop an action plan tailored to fit your specific needs.

Let's get the conversation started.

Call 888.763.9045 today.

solution-tree.com